Net Profit

Best wishes,

Further praise for *Net Profit*

"A readable, up-to-date and highly practical guide to running a successful e-business."
John Quelch – Lincoln Filene Professor of Business Administration, Harvard Business School

"Soskin is something of a Godfather to Britain's digital economy. So Net Profit *is an essential read for anyone looking to start or improve their internet offerings."*
Ian Wallis – Editor, *Growing Business Magazine*

"Real words of wisdom from someone who can explain both 'the forest' and 'the trees' based on experience. Net Profit *offers priceless advice not just for digital entrepreneurs but also for any executive or professional with an interest in the digital economy."*
Dan Bricklin – Co-creator of VisiCalc, the pioneering electronic spreadsheet, and author of *Bricklin on Technology*

"Really practical advice from someone who has been there and done it! Soskin's deep experience of what works and what doesn't work for internet businesses shines through on every page. A fascinating read with hugely valuable insights for e-entrepreneurs."
Adrian Beecroft – Founder, former Chief Investment Officer and Senior Managing Partner, Apax Partners

Net Profit

How to Succeed in Digital Business

David Soskin

A John Wiley & Sons, Ltd., Publication

This edition first published 2010
Copyright © 2010 David Soskin

Registered office
John Wiley & Sons Ltd, The Atrium, Southern Gate, Chichester, West Sussex, PO19 8SQ,
United Kingdom

For details of our global editorial offices, for customer services and for information about how
to apply for permission to reuse the copyright material in this book please see our website at
www.wiley.com.

The right of the author to be identified as the author of this work has been asserted in
accordance with the Copyright, Designs and Patents Act 1988.

Wiley also publishes its books in a variety of electronic formats. Some content that appears in
print may not be available in electronic books.

Designations used by companies to distinguish their products are often claimed as trademarks.
All brand names and product names used in this book are trade names, service marks,
trademarks or registered trademarks of their respective owners. The publisher is not associated
with any product or vendor mentioned in this book. This publication is designed to provide
accurate and authoritative information in regard to the subject matter covered. It is sold on the
understanding that the publisher is not engaged in rendering professional services. If
professional advice or other expert assistance is required, the services of a competent
professional should be sought.

Library of Congress Cataloging-in-Publication Data

Soskin, David, 1954-
    Net profit : the secrets of success in digital business / David Soskin.
      p. cm.
    Includes bibliographical references and index.
    ISBN 978-0-470-66081-2 (pbk.)
    1. Electronic commerce.   2. Success in business.   I. Title.
    HF5548.32.S644 2010
    658.8'72—dc22
                                                                2010021965

A catalogue record for this book is available from the British Library.

ISBN 978-0-470-66081-2 (hardback), ISBN 978-0-470-97334-9 (ebk),
ISBN 978-0-470-97134-5 (ebk), ISBN 978-0-470-97135-2 (ebk)

Typeset in 11/16pt Janson MT by Toppan Best-set Premedia Limited, Hong Kong
Printed in Great Britain by TJ International Ltd, Padstow, Cornwall, UK

For Alexandra

CONTENTS

ACKNOWLEDGEMENTS

First, I would like to thank Ellen Hallsworth of John Wiley & Sons whose idea this book was and who gave me the green light. She has been patient with me at every stage and her rigorous editing has helped transform an internet entrepreneur's thoughts into a book.

John Hatt and Hugo Burge kindly took the time to read an early draft. I am deeply grateful to them for their sage advice.

This book would not have been possible without the expertise of many colleagues past and present including John Barrington-Carver, Milenko Beslic, Ceri Davies, Shahin Fard, Brian Fitzgerald, Tom Impallomeni, Suzanne Lilley, Christian Lindstrom, Kam Rai and Jonny Steel. They are all stars of the digital firmament.

Dan Bricklin and Nicholas Negroponte were my muses. They were the earliest of 'early adopters' and they were among the very first to predict the digital revolution. I appreciate their wise counsel.

Jonathan Cornthwaite, a partner of Wedlake Bell, took the time not only to read and critique my early drafts but also to advise me on the complex issue of intellectual property, a subject in which he is a leading expert. I could not have had a better guide. Angela

Mansi of WorkLife Management likewise gave me some valuable comments on my 'People' chapter.

The life of an entrepreneur can often feel lonely; so talking to other entrepreneurs can be both reassuring and encouraging as many issues are common across different businesses. One entrepreneur in particular whom I would like to thank is the enormously talented Victor van Amerongen, who has been a great friend since my Oxford days and whose comments about this book have been very helpful.

I must thank the CEOs and founders of the companies in which Howzat Media has invested. I have watched with admiration as they have expanded their respective companies and they are a great group: in the UK, Peter Ward and Jerome Touze of WAYN and Sokratis Papafloratos of TrustedPlaces; in Germany, Rolf Schrömgens, Peter Vinnemeier and Malte Siewert of Trivago; and, in the USA, Chris Hill of CheapToday and Richard Price of Academia.

I would also like to thank the internet CEOs and founders who have given me their valuable time, especially Hugh Chappell of TrustedReviews and Richard Moross of Moo.

Linda Pilkington, founder of Ormonde Jayne, gave me a useful insight into how her website has helped successfully grow her perfumery enterprise, and I am grateful to her for this.

I must mention two members of my media team at ABN AMRO, Harjinder Singh-Heer and Raiko Mancini. We worked closely together exploring the dynamics of a then nascent digital industry. We learned much together.

My own circle of friends and family includes some avid readers who have helpfully shared with me over the years their views as to what makes for a 'good read', especially Simon Clark, Keith Gregory, David Roodyn and Shirley Soskin.

My excellent editor at *Growing Business Magazine*, James Hurley, has been rightly demanding with his deadlines but always resolute in his support. James got me writing again after a long absence.

Susan and Han Alloun, Ross McInnes and Jerome Bourreau were all immensely generous with their hospitality, allowing me to stay at their fine houses in France while I constructed the shape of the manuscript.

I have talked to a lot of people in the vibrant and growing London internet community while writing this book – too many to list here but I do thank you all.

Most importantly of all, I am indebted to my wife Alexandra to whom this book is dedicated. Alexandra read all my drafts and her comments, critique and support were invaluable. My love and gratitude, as ever.

David Soskin
London, 2010

PREFACE

Back in 1994, I returned to the campus of Harvard Business School to attend my 15th reunion weekend. These reunions are held every five years. They act as networking events designed both to keep graduates in touch with each other and for Harvard Business School to ensure that its fundraising activities enable it to remain as one of the best-endowed academic institutions in the history of mankind. Part social, part study, the reunions are always well attended.

The welcome party, held on the sun-dappled lawns outside the school's imposing Baker Library, was the first opportunity to greet my classmates, many of whom I had not seen in the 15 years since graduation. I immediately spotted Dan Bricklin. Though he no longer sported a pony tail, he was still dressed in the same uniform of faded jeans and a tee shirt that he had worn throughout his two years of classes.

Twelve years earlier, and just three years after graduating from the Harvard Business School, Dan had been named by *Time* magazine as runner-up for their Man of the Year Award. His financial spreadsheet Visicalc was certainly one of the most important software inventions in history. Not only did it turbo-charge the growth of the personal computer, it revolutionized the ability of business everywhere to plan and to model.

Dan was asked to moderate a panel discussion at this reunion. The subject was 'Cruising the Information Superhighway'. The other panel on offer was 'Buyouts and Industry Restructuring'. For me, this was like the movie *Sliding Doors*, the plot of which revolves around the slightest happenstance providing a life-changing moment. Maybe if I had opted for the other panel discussion, my career would have been very different. And I would almost certainly not be writing this book.

Happily (for me), as Dan was a friend and I was fascinated by the Visicalc story, I decided to opt for his session, albeit with some trepidation. I imagined that the complexity of its content (brainy Dan had inevitably done his Bachelor's degree in Electrical Engineering and Computer Science at MIT, the Massachusetts Institute of Technology) would prove too much for my liberal arts-trained mind.

So it was that at 9.20am on Saturday 4 June 1994, I joined the audience in the austere, windowless surroundings of Aldrich Room 109. I do not recall what the other panellists said. But I do recall Dan's dazzling performance. He gazed into a future where digital technology would revolutionize the world. He argued in the plainest of terms that we were going to see it transform society.

He talked of course about the 'Information Superhighway' (the original name for the internet) and gave example after example of what the future would look like. He described how a motoring accident would be attended by paramedics able to receive expert guidance from a top surgeon supervising their work, in real time, aided by screen images sent via a digital camera. He talked too about something called an 'internet browser'. He explained this was a device enabling anyone to find what they wanted on the World Wide Web quickly and easily. It was called 'Mosaic' and had been developed over the previous couple of years by Marc Andreessen.

Many business careers move ahead in a straight line: you get a promotion; you manage more people; you are allocated a bigger budget. But there are few 'light bulb' moments. For me, after listening to one of America's most celebrated technology stars spell out his vision of the future, in the very place where, 15 years earlier, I had completed my MBA, life would never be the same again. The light bulb was switched on and burning brightly.

I was determined then to understand this digital revolution better and to see if there was within it a business opportunity for me. What excited me more than anything was the prediction that it could change forever the way we consume media. For I had been fascinated by the media from a very young age.

To take the story back a bit, some of my earliest childhood memories are of my regular weekly visits to the *Observer* newspaper, the oldest Sunday newspaper in the world (founded in 1791). It was then headquartered in a vast block which it shared with *The Times* in Blackfriars near to the River Thames. My aunt was the *Observer*'s political correspondent and, on Saturdays, she used regularly to invite me to see the paper being 'put to bed'. The print room, the rolling presses, the photographic 'dark rooms', the erudite conversation among the paper's journalists, all carried out under the direction of the charismatic editor and proprietor David Astor, gave me a taste for media which I never lost.

Years later, on going to Oxford University, I immediately joined the staff of *The Cherwell*, the student newspaper. There I progressed from advertising sales manager (this, in the main, required visiting Chinese restaurants and not leaving without a cheque for the advertisements they had been placing all term – an early lesson in income recognition and cash management) to general manager and then to director of Oxford Student Publications Limited, the parent company of *The Cherwell*, on which board I sat for nearly three years.

After Oxford, and my Harvard MBA, my career was diverse, often hovering around the edges of the media industry. I worked for Redland, an international construction products company, and was involved in a consortium which applied for local and national TV franchises – I was unable to rid myself of the media bug.

In the 1990s, I worked as a policy adviser to Prime Minister John Major in Number 10 Downing Street. Whilst there, scribbling policy papers, I often thought about Dan Bricklin and his predictions. Then a friend, a TV producer, gave me a book which he said was a 'must read'. Called *Being Digital*, its author was the founder of the Media Laboratory at MIT, Nicholas Negroponte. Like Dan, he too predicted the future. In the intervening decade and a half since the book was published, much of what he foresaw has actually happened.

To take just one example: Negroponte predicted in the book that paper would be replaced by screens and that books as we know them would be superseded by electronic reading tablets. Fast forward to 2010 when Kindles, Sony E-readers, iPads and other electronic book devices are already being sold the world over by the truckload. As I read the book, I thought of my own experience in the TV world and of that newspaper print room of my childhood. The world was about to change and I wanted to be part of that change. By early 2000 I had achieved my goal. I found myself at Cheapflights sitting in a tiny room in Wandsworth, South London, above Foxtons the estate agents. We had just £20,000 in the bank, and the team was small – just three of us.

Just a few weeks before, I had been running ABN AMRO's global media team. At that time, ABN AMRO had over 100,000 employees, with 12,000 in the investment banking division alone. The London office where I worked was a vast green plate-glass edifice shaped, rather appropriately, like a slice of Dutch Gouda cheese. It was three years since I had joined ABN AMRO, and I was yearning to get into the digital economy.

But none of the many new digital ventures at which I had been looking appealed to me. They all seemed to have fatal flaws: inexperienced, weak management (not that there were many experienced digital executives in the late 1990s) and too many young people with lots of energy and creative input but little or no idea about either business or the sectors which they planned to conquer. Worse, the plans called for huge amounts of cash. $100m was a common number. Why $100m? I do not know. It was a nice fat, round number. That was about it.

To compound the problems, none of these companies seemed to be able to make money any time soon – the common model was emerging as one of years of losses before arriving at the eventual promised land of profits.

By late 1999, I was feeling a bit despondent about finding the right internet opportunity.

And that's when I received a telephone call from an old friend. '*David*', he said. '*Look, I can't really talk. I am at a funeral and they are just about to bury the deceased. But there is someone here I have been chatting to. He is called John Hatt. He owns a company called Cheapflights and he wants to sell it.*'

From the graveside to the birth of a new career.

Well, you need a bit of luck in this world.

ABOUT THE AUTHOR

David Soskin is a seasoned internet entrepreneur and business commentator.

Currently Chairman of mySupermarket.co.uk and of Swapit.co.uk, David was, for eight years, CEO of Cheapflights Media and remains on its board of directors. In that time he grew the groundbreaking company from an attic-based operation into an award-winning international leader in online travel search with tens of millions of users worldwide.

David is also co-founder of Howzat Media LLP, which invests in early-stage digital media companies on both sides of the Atlantic.

He is a regular speaker on the subject of internet business and writes a monthly column in *Growing Business Magazine.*

Prior to Cheapflights, David held senior roles in industry, banking and government.

He was educated at Oxford University and the Harvard Business School. David is married and lives in London.

INTRODUCTION

You may have shied away from starting an internet business because you fear that you do not have the technology skills; or that you need a lot of money to get started; or that internet businesses are by definition loss-making; or that you are simply too old. Shed your misgivings. I will show in this book that this is not only an excellent time to start an internet business, it is also much more possible than perhaps you might think.

I have written the book around eight key themes:

- The commercial internet's early years and what can be learned from them
- The central role of the customer even in the digital world and how different types of revenue models continue to multiply
- The importance of building a great team
- The product and how crucial it is to get the website right
- Raising money, prudent financial management and exits
- Driving traffic
- The global potential offered to businesses by the massive expansion of the internet
- The future

Some of what I say may seem blindingly obvious. I anticipate that some sophisticates of the blogosphere might take issue, for instance, with anyone writing in 2010 about the need to get the website right.

But I know from personal experience just how many really bad websites remain – and that has nothing to do with cash. I have seen small business websites with better design, look and feel and functionality than some of those owned by major companies.

I have written this book primarily for entrepreneurs either running internet businesses, or considering doing so, and wanting those businesses to be profitable. I hope that it will be useful too for all those in the digital economy who seek a broader understanding of some of the areas with which they may not be familiar. You may be expert at optimizing your website for search engines but not fully comprehend the importance of cash conservation. You may be a virtuoso at selling online advertising but not grasp fully the necessity of good web design. You may be a business whizz in your own domestic market but not have experienced the pitfalls of building a cross-border business. So I hope this book will be useful if you wish to broaden your skill base as you build your career in the digital economy.

It is a good time to start up, to work and to invest in the digital economy. Unlike so many economic activities, digital business continued to grow throughout the 2007–2009 credit crunch. Internet technology allowed hard-pressed consumers to compare prices and save money. It continued to provide a major catalyst to the way people conduct business in the old economy. In this book I show some examples ranging from a luxury one-shop per-fumier in Mayfair who uses the internet to tap the global market to the mighty supermarket company Tesco with its vast online investment.

Retailing, search, price comparison, consumer reviews, music and video are just some of the areas which have been transformed by the digital economy in just 15 years.

The digital revolution is engulfing the world's population. The internet is here to stay. The top four internet companies (all American) have a market value of $300bn. New companies are becoming global operations at breakneck speed. Twitter, Face-book, Spotify and many others have been launched in this new century and are already used by hundreds of millions. It is now a cliché that if Facebook was a country it would be one of the world's largest.

For the younger generation in particular the internet is the first port of call for a range of activities including research and shopping. They are the first 'digital natives' whose knowledge was recently proven when a 15-year-old intern at the investment bank Morgan Stanley wrote a research note on internet usage that became one of the most widely-circulated research papers in its history.

So this is good news for anyone considering launching an internet business. It is not too late. Quite the opposite in fact for the inter-net is still in its infancy. The market is growing. Young people, the consumers of the future, are by definition practically all inter-net users. The opportunities are vast.

And the great internet ideas have, in the main, come from individuals not huge companies. Even the legions employed by media über-mogul Rupert Murdoch have not so far come up with a single world-beating internet idea. Murdoch resorted to buying MySpace and the jury is still out on just how successful that purchase really was. Amazon was invented by Jeff Bezos: it did not derive from bookseller giants like Barnes & Noble or Borders. CraigsList.com, which has singlehandedly swung a wrecking-ball through the classified advertising revenues of the great traditional media juggernauts, was the brainchild of San Francisco-based Craig Newmark.

In this book, I cite examples from the first 15 or so years of the internet's commercial life. These examples are to illustrate some of the do's and don't's of the internet business and to draw more clearly practical lessons from the experience of others. There is, however, nothing more compelling than first-hand experience. You will notice very soon that I talk a lot about Cheapflights. I trust that you will excuse me for doing so. Cheapflights is the internet company that I came across in late 1999, I ran for eight years and on whose board I still sit. So I know the company and the experience of building it intimately. It provides some good lessons for any entrepreneur anywhere in the world seeking to start and grow a successful digital business.

Just like the Cheapflights website, the book is intended to be accessible to all, not just the 'digerati'. The purpose of the book is to share some of basic rules of running a successful digital media company. Much of it is plain common business sense: the advent of the World Wide Web does not mean that traditional methodology has suddenly died.

I hope the book will become a basic primer for the digital media industry and that it will destroy many of the canards that have become so prevalent. For example, to succeed, you do not (necessarily) need:

- Millions of pounds of investment;
- A computer science degree from MIT;
- A Silicon Valley HQ;
- To be 22 years old;
- Ever to lose money;
- To spend a fortune on advertising.

You do need a great idea, super people, a sound business plan, energy and tenacity.

Chapter One

THE DIGITAL REVOLUTION – A SHORT HISTORY

'*Lo*' (the first word ever to be transmitted on the ARPANet, precursor to the internet, 29 October 1969)

I've written this book to help you build a successful digital business. First, though, it is important to understand why and how this revolution happened in order better to grasp today's business opportunities.

The forefathers of the internet saw a time when the entire world would be linked up. Is it surprising then that some of today's largest internet businesses such as Facebook have built themselves on this aspiration? Because the internet is an inherently global medium, it has enabled the sort of explosive growth that has witnessed companies like Amazon, Yahoo, eBay and Google go from nothing to major international players within the space of less than two decades. At no time in the history of business have there ever been global businesses created quite so quickly.

By understanding the milestones that led to the commercial internet – and the progress of the World Wide Web since that time – entrepreneurs can appreciate more keenly that the pace of change has been relentless and it is speeding up, not slowing down. Each change leads to more and more opportunities for the agile and imaginative entrepreneur.

This chapter looks at the formative years of the internet, the huge hopes that accompanied the early pioneers and the dramatic crash that followed. For those in the digital economy, or planning to join it, there are lessons to be learned from those early failures and of course from those companies that survived the meltdown to thrive and prosper.

Origins of the internet

There was no Eureka moment for the internet.

So how had the technology evolved? Over the three decades from the 1960s, the internet emerged out of an alphabet soup, as ARPANet was followed by CSNET and finally NSFNET.

First ARPANet. In 1957 the USA was in a state of collective shock. The Russians had launched their first satellite, the Sputnik, into space. President Eisenhower was determined that it would be the USA and not the USSR that would lead the world in technology. So he created ARPA – the United States Department of Defense Advanced Research Projects Agency – to fund research into advanced technology. Among ARPA's areas of focus was computer research.

An early key figure at ARPA was MIT Professor Joseph Carl Robnett 'Lick' Licklider. Licklider foresaw a time when everyone on the globe would be interconnected. Anyone could access information at any computer from anywhere. With a good interface and strong computing capability, ideas and performance would flourish. This was the conception of today's internet. It would take another three and a half decades before Licklider's vision became a reality and the internet would indeed become a global phenomenon.

ARPA regarded the need to link up the recipients of its research dollars as a priority. All over the USA, ARPA was funding centres of excellence: UCLA had simulation; the University of Utah, graphics; the University of Illinois, high performance computers. How could all these brilliant researchers communicate with each other and exchange ideas?

The key to the construction of a network was packet switching technology whereby relatively small units of data ('packets') could be routed between computers through a network based on the destination address contained within each packet. Breaking communication down into packets allowed the same data path to be shared by many users in the network. Packet switching is, of course, the basic technology behind the internet.

On 29 October 1969, ARPANet was established in California between UCLA and the Stanford Research Institute. The first message which was meant to be transmitted was '*login*' but the system crashed midstream, so only '*lo*' was received; a more biblical than technical debut.

The launch of ARPANet did not attract the publicity that accompanied Neil Armstrong's first steps on the moon only three months before; but, for mankind, it may have been an even greater leap.

In the 1970s, the use of computers became more and more wide-spread, propelled by 'Moore's Law'. Coined by Intel co-founder Gordon Moore in 1965, it states that the number of transistors on a chip doubles every 24 months.

We have seen how, in 1969, ARPANet led the way in networking computers. But access to it was not universal, being confined to government and academic researchers.

In 1981, the National Science Foundation (NSF) – an American federally-funded agency which supports non-medical research and education in science and engineering – started its own network called the 'Computer Science Network' or CSNET. This system connected to the ARPANet and provided internet services, including email. It was also international, linking the USA to many countries in Europe and Asia. This widened the user base considerably. But it was not, as yet, the mass application that we know today.[1]

Two years later, in 1983, there was another important advance. Paul Mockapetris invented the Domain Name System, more commonly known as '.com', '.co.uk', '.org', and other popular suffixes.[2] The Domain Name System is the 'phone book' for the internet which translates human-friendly computer hostnames into Internet Protocol (IP) addresses. For example, *www.example.com* translates to *208.77.188.166*.

In 1985, the NSF began funding the creation of five new super-computer centres. The National Science Foundation Network or NSFNET connected these five centres and allowed access to their supercomputers over the network at no cost. From then until the advent of a commercialized internet 10 years later, the NSFNET was the principal internet backbone (CSNET was eventually phased out).[3]

The World Wide Web

Now the story moves to Europe, specifically to the Franco-Swiss border near Geneva and the European Organization for Nuclear Research, better known by its French acronym CERN.

It was here that an Englishman and Oxford physics graduate, Tim Berners-Lee (now Sir Tim), invented the World Wide Web (www). This development was, of course, critical to the commercialization of the internet. It was to the internet a development of the same magnitude as Gutenberg's printing press was to the publishing industry. It is a system of interlinked 'hypertext' documents accessed via the internet. Hypertext (which had been invented all the way back in 1965) is text displayed on a computer with references (hyperlinks) to other text that the reader can immediately access, usually by clicking. Apart from running text, hypertext may contain tables, images and other presentational devices. Berners-Lee's breakthrough was the hyperlink which allowed users to 'link' from one document to the next.

The first website, 'Info.cern.ch', went online on 6 August 1991. Its address was http://info.cern.ch/hypertext/WWW/TheProject.html and it described the WWW project.[4]

There is an interesting postscript to the invention of the World Wide Web. For even as distinguished a scientist as Berners-Lee could make mistakes. In 2009, he admitted that the infuriating double forward slashes that precede every website address were unnecessary. *'Really, if you think about it, it doesn't need the //'*, he told a symposium. *'I could have designed it not to have the //.'*[5]

For around 20 years, the internet had been largely the preserve of scientists, academics, researchers and computer geeks of all sorts. Thanks to Berners-Lee's invention of the World Wide Web in 1991, it was now open house. The number of internet users jumped from 600,000 to 50 million in just four years.

The other key driver of the early internet was the improving 'web browsers' which Dan Bricklin had described in his June 1994 Harvard talk. These built on Berners-Lee's WWW invention. Better web browsers meant more easily retrieving and navigating information on the World Wide Web. Celebrated though it is, the Mosaic browser was predated by many others (such as Cello and ViolaWWW), now sadly forgotten by most people. What made Mosaic so different was that it was more user-friendly than its predecessors.

The development of the internet in the 1960s and the subsequent invention both of the World Wide Web and of improving browsers in the 1990s contributed to a true communications revolution.

Of course, communications revolutions do happen – but not all that often. According to one scholar of ancient civilizations, Lord Sachs, the Chief Rabbi of the United Kingdom, there have been four watersheds in people's ability to communicate with one another.

The first was the invention of writing in ancient Mesopotamia; the second was the invention of the alphabet; the third was the development of the 'codex', the book as a set of bound pages rather than a scroll; the fourth was, of course, the invention of printing in the mid-fifteenth century.[6]

And now, in our own time, we have the fifth revolution, the internet, which at the time of writing is used by 1.7 billion users. Put simply, this means that one in every four humans in the world is an internet user.[7]

No new technology has ever been adopted so quickly. It took four years to attract the first 50 million internet users compared with 38 years for radio, 16 years for the personal computer and 13 years for television.[8]

The business of the internet begins

The National Science Foundation Network (NSFNET) had until 1993 an 'Acceptable Use Policy' prohibiting commercial use of the internet. Now the policy was dropped. The internet had, for the first time, moved from 'not for profit' into the world of free market capitalism.

Taking advantage of this liberalization, Tim O'Reilly, the founder and CEO of O'Reilly Media and one of the USA's foremost commentators on technology, launched Global Network Navigator (GNN), an 'Internet-based Information Center', in August 1993. O'Reilly argues that GNN was the first commercial website, the first to introduce the portal concept, and the first use of internet advertising as a business model.[9]

This was a moment comparable to the birth of the modern oil industry. Oil had been around for a long time (millions of years in fact); but its monetary value was limited because its commercial applications were few. Then, in the nineteenth century, it became a staple for lighting and heating and, of course, for the combustion engine. Fortunes were made. At the beginning of the twentieth century, Standard Oil of New Jersey was so large that the US government broke it up. Nevertheless its offshoot Exxon became one of the world's largest corporations as did its rivals BP and Shell.

Similarly, the internet had been around for a while as a communication tool. Then, suddenly, the internet was not just a place for communication but a place where money could be made. And internet advertising became to the end of the twentieth century just what oil was to the end of the nineteenth century. The same excitement, the same hype, the same triumphs, the same disasters and some similar 'new industry' dynamics played out – like the early combustion engine and the far-reaching implications of motorized road transport.

Early entrants

Many of today's biggest internet success stories date from the earliest days of the internet's post-1993 commercialization (Amazon and Yahoo were founded in 1994, eBay in 1995 and Google in 1998). I will look at the lessons these teach us about building successful businesses. But it is also useful to look at the early failures and the reasons for their demise.

It is quite true that many of the early players that once promised so much fell apart. Who today remembers Alta Vista (founded 1995), once one of the world's leading search engines; Webvan (founded 1996), which promised to bring groceries ordered online to the door of every PC user; or Value America (also founded in 1996), which promised 'convergence commerce', the opportunity for American shoppers to buy online directly from manufacturers?

Why did they all fail? Each was for a different reason, but their respective collapses serve as clear warnings to anyone wanting to start or grow an internet business.

The search engine Alta Vista (which means 'a view from above') was one of the most popular websites in America. Its failure stemmed from an unwise diversification. It decided that it wanted to be a portal as well, competing head-on in unfamiliar territory, with Yahoo and others. In so doing, Alta Vista strayed from its core competence (search). Not only did Alta Vista fail to compete successfully as a portal, but as management focused on this, they took their eye off the search ball. This allowed the search industry's new kid on the block Google (which launched in 1998, a full three years after Alta Vista) to beat them at their core competence. Alta Vista was finally acquired in February 2003 by Overture Inc. for a knockdown price of $140m, compared to its valuation of $2.3bn three years previously.

Another exemplary failure was Webvan, an online grocery shop, which flew too close to the sun before reality caught up with it. Founded by the bookshop entrepreneur Louis Borders, it had ambitious plans to roll out across the whole of the USA. It recruited ex-Andersen Consulting CEO George Shaheen as CEO and, in 1999, things looked peachy. After a successful Initial Public Offering (IPO), its market value reached almost $6bn.

Innocent days. And it is quite understandable that, in those days of internet infancy, observers were all so focused on the dreams that they overlooked the obvious shortcomings of the business plan. Webvan had several fairly clear weaknesses. No one spotted or cared very much that the founder was not in fact a grocery guy. Nor that its sales (just a few million dollars) were miniscule. Nor that it was untested beyond precisely one city (San Francisco). Nor that its CEO was a management consultant. With a $6bn valuation, who wanted to be a party pooper?

In 2001, just a year and a half after its remarkably successful IPO, Webvan closed all its operations and filed for Chapter 11 bankruptcy protection. It had been far too optimistic about people's willingness to give up their traditional ways of shopping in favour of something new and different. It had overinvested in something that was quite untested.

As the magazine *Wired* pointed out rather sourly:

> *This type of extreme optimism was pervasive in late 1999, when Webvan went public.*[10]

As for Value America, its IPO in April 1999 was also a huge success. It raised $115m with an offering price of $23. On the first day of trading, its shares opened at $63 and closed at $55, valuing the three-year-old, profitless, company at a heady $2.4bn.

In that same year, the respected Forrester Research Inc. ranked Value America fourth in its league of general merchandise e-commerce sites, behind Amazon.com, Wal-Mart and QVC. Forrester noted in October that the company's *'low prices compensated for numerous site design problems'*![11]

Value America's founder, the inappropriately named Craig Winn, could certainly talk the talk. A local business magazine took up the story:

> *'You've got to hear the sermon. Craig Winn is a little like an evangelist. After you hear him talk, you almost want to give him money',*

says Alfred C. Weaver, a computer science professor at the University of Virginia.

Some have done just that. Co-founder Rex Scatena, an environmental lawyer, provided start-up funding and now serves as Vice Chairman and General Counsel. Ken Power, Value America's creative director, says that within the company, they have a name for this intoxication: 'drinking the Kool-Aid.' He's among the imbibers.[12]

Apparently Winn drank so much of his own Kool Aid that he seriously considered having a crack at the Presidency of the United States.

But behind the scenes chaos reigned as described in a side-splitting (unless of course you had been an investor) account of the company's rapid fall in *Dot.Bomb* by J. David Kuo, who worked for Value America. The information systems were never properly built; shipments and deliveries were a disaster; shareholders' money was lavished on private jets; and an elaborate office 'campus' was built in Virginia.

In the end, it was not the White House that beckoned Winn but rather an ignominious retreat to Chapter 11 of the Bankruptcy Code.

What is interesting about these three collapses was that in each case there was a fundamental problem which investors were simply too inexperienced and overexcited to spot.

Alta Vista made the fatal error of straying from its core mission of search into territory better understood by others (advertising-based portals), allowing upstart Google to develop a world-beating search product that destroyed Alta Vista's ability to compete – an early lesson of the breakneck speed at which internet commerce operates.

Webvan hastily invested its shareholders' money in a vast infrastructure that was completely unsuited for the modest demand for its product.[13] It overexpanded. At that time, there was low internet penetration and limited experience of online shopping. Consumers do not change their grocery buying habits overnight.

Ten years on it is the UK that is now the most advanced online grocery shopping market in the world (where probably well in excess of $2bn has been invested by companies such as Tesco, ASDA and Ocado). Yet still fewer than 3% of overall British grocery sales are online[14] and that is in a country that enjoys 80% internet access.

The subsequent British experience shows that actually Webvan was not a bad idea – just a company whose idea was perhaps 20 years ahead of its time.

Value America talked the talk but failed to walk the walk. Like Craig Winn, Amazon CEO Jeff Bezos is a great salesman; but anyone who uses Amazon knows that much of its success is in the detail of execution – from the design of its website and the packaging of its goods, to its highly sophisticated customer relationship management. In stark contrast, it seems that Value America's operations management bordered on the farcical.

Surviving the 'dot.com crash'

The internet revolution has only just started. The commercial internet is barely 15 years old. We are only just beginning to comprehend its power as a communications tool and its capacity to underpin successful business models.

Yet already the industry has been written off once during a difficult period called, rather prematurely, 'the dot.com collapse'. In 2000–2002, following a wave of business failures, many pundits were suggesting that the whole thing was just a flash in the pan, just like Tulipmania (a grotesque speculation in the price of tulips in seventeenth-century Netherlands) and the South Sea Bubble (a wild speculation on the shares of the South Sea Company in eighteenth-century Britain based on a fallacious belief in the exponential growth of trade with the New World).

In reality, however, this was nothing more sinister than some adolescent problems: overhyped business plans, inexperienced management, limited user access, the slow performance and high cost of internet use (those wretched dial-up charges!) – and, of course, the bubble element, a surfeit of investor exuberance. Naysayers and overexuberance often go hand in hand – in the 1890s, many people wrote off the horseless carriage as accident-prone, overhyped, too expensive and doomed to fail.

The so-called dot.com crash wiped out $5tn in the market value of technology companies from March 2000 to October 2002. Opinions differ as to why the fall happened so fast and on such a huge scale: disappointing online retailing results from the 1999 Christmas trading period; Microsoft's anti-trust hearings; a huge one-off technology spend on the Y2K (the millennium bug) switchover; and enormous, simultaneous sell orders for leading tech stocks such as IBM and Cisco. All have been cited as contributors to the collapse.

In fact, much of the financial disaster related not to dot.coms but to the failure of the big telecoms infrastructure firms such as WorldCom, a company which was riddled with fraud. It overstated its assets by billions of dollars and its CEO Bernie Ebbers was later sentenced to 25 years in prison. Much of that 'lost cash' from the pre-bubble era went into the creation of long-haul fibre optic systems and local networks which provide the backbone for today's internet companies.

It was not just big names that went down in the dot.com 'collapse'. Hundreds of small companies disappeared. They were out of cash and the funding dried up. The UK had its fair share of disasters. Who remembers now ClickMango, an online health and beauty e-tailer backed by Atlas Ventures and the Rothschild Family Trust and fronted by TV star Joanna Lumley? Or Ready2shop.com, a fashion advice business co-founded in November 1999 by fashion gurus Trinny Woodall and Susannah Constantine? Or Beenz.com which allowed consumers to earn 'beenz' (a type of online currency, for performing activities such as visiting a website, shopping online, or logging on) which raised almost $100m from blue-chip investors including Apax, Larry Ellison of Oracle, and Francois Pinault of PPR? Hardly surprising then that the internet industry rapidly became a byword for failure and incompetence.

Many of these businesses were simply launched too early. For in the UK, in the late 1990s, internet access was not universal. In 1999, at the height of the euphoria, internet penetration was 13% (barely one in 10 homes). People at home were spending on average only eight hours a month (480 minutes) online – 16 minutes a day! But the most staggering statistic is this: internet advertising in total was barely £50m.

A decade ago technology costs were high, dial-up internet access was the norm (imagine paying by the minute for the time spent online) and many people were simply too frightened to put their credit card details into a computer.

However, recent research suggests that as many as 50% of the dot.coms survived the trough, reflecting two facts: first, the destruction of public market wealth did not necessarily correspond to companies going out of business; and second, that most of the dot.coms were small players who in fact weathered the financial markets storm.[15] These were companies that had genuinely robust business models, had not overextended themselves financially, had kept costs under control, were monetizing effectively and had the good fortune to find themselves in a business sector that fitted well with the internet's then limited capability and reach.

It is worth emphasizing that today's largest internet companies (namely Google, Amazon, eBay and Yahoo) – not to mention scores of others – were all founded well *before* the dot.com 'collapse'. Some businesses, unlike general online retailing, were well suited even to the limited demand of the internet's earliest years. The travel sector was an early adopter thanks in part to the low-cost airlines who made online booking an early priority. That helped newly-floated online travel companies like the UK's LastMinute and eBookers ride the stock market storm.

The key point here is that the industry was simply going through its first phase of consolidation. Those looking at US car manufacturers in the 1890s might have judged it a frail industry, not one which presaged a century of explosive global growth. Who remembers the early car entrepreneurs Elwood Haynes, Alexander Winton, or the brothers Charles Edgar and Frank Duryea? But, just like Henry Ford of the early car industry, several of the pioneering 'dot.coms' founders not only survived but went on to become world-beaters.

While it was true that many early predictions of commercial success were wildly optimistic, many leading media analysts (including Mary Meeker and Henry Blodget) who were so pilloried at the time were onto something.

The top four quoted internet companies – Google, eBay, Yahoo and Amazon – have a combined market capitalization of nearly $300bn. Fifteen years ago this industry did not exist. This must be some of the fastest shareholder value ever created.

Old economy companies, often led by executives cruelly dubbed by former Wall Street analyst Henry Blodget as 'Digital Dunces', are stumbling into the future as the pace of change accelerates. Increasingly they realize that a digital strategy is not an option, but a must. For many traditional media companies, that realization has come 10 years too late. So how did those early internet giants, the victors of the first decade of serious internet usage succeed while so many others failed?

Early entrants: lessons for commercial success

Each of the early successes identified an application for which digital technology was especially well suited, and implemented that idea brilliantly. They delighted their users with the excellence of their products. They created a buzz around their websites which meant that expensive offline advertising was unnecessary. They did something that the traditional economy could not do. And, crucially, each found a way to monetize its product so that, as traffic grew, so did sales and profits. Interestingly, they were not necessarily the ones to have the original ideas.

Google and search

Today Google is the largest media company in the world. Valued at $170bn, it dwarfs old economy behemoths such as Time Warner ($36bn) and Rupert Murdoch's News Corp ($30bn) despite their ambitious forays into new media.

Google, incorporated in September 1998, reached these giddy heights owing to its invention of an algorithmic-based search engine backed by 'AdWords'. These 'AdWords', if bid for, can automatically generate the tastefully-termed 'sponsored links' arranged vertically above and next to the free search results.

Google did not invent either the free search engine or the 'paid-for' search model (the 'pay-per-click' search engine or, as Google's version is called, 'AdWords'). Free search engines were, from the outset, one of the internet's hottest sectors. At least 16 search engines had been launched before Google went live in 1998. Magellan, Excite, Infoseek, Yahoo and others were already battling for supremacy with Alta Vista which had over half the US market by 1998.

Open Text came up with the idea of 'pay-per-click' advertising as early as 1996. But this caused a public outcry as the early internet adopters did not want the search process 'contaminated' by paid-for results.[16]

Within the next couple of years, internet commerce had taken off and users were much more tolerant of the new media's advertising applications. That was when the first major commercialized 'pay-per-click' search engine was conceived by Bill Gross, the founder of the business 'incubator' Idealab. (An incubator is an enterprise that is set up to provide office space, equipment and assistance to start-ups.)

The company that developed this idea was founded by Gross in early 1998, GoTo.com Inc. This was the first successful company to provide an internet search engine that relied on sponsored search results and pay-per-click advertisements. Gross discovered that growing numbers of internet users did not mind searches that were influenced by payment or the appearance of sponsored messages any more than they would refuse to read far less targeted newspaper advertisements or watch TV commercials. GoTo.com was later renamed Overture Services Inc. and was then acquired by Yahoo in 2003 for $1.3bn to provide its Yahoo Search Marketing products.

Bill Gross's idea was simplicity itself: 'Sponsored Search', where advertisers only pay *when their ad is clicked*. This one simple idea was to undermine the revenue model of the world's mightiest media companies. Newspapers, radio, TV: they had no idea what was going to hit them. The shark of online advertising was swimming rapidly towards the shore while complacent traditional media executives splashed happily in the shallow waters. They were oblivious to the impending threat. The shark ultimately would not just eat their lunch, it would eat them too.

But now both Alta Vista, the world's first major search engine, and GoTo, which pioneered pay-per-click, are largely forgotten. By 2008, Google accounted for over 80% of the world's searches, and its founders Sergey Brin and Larry Page are feted the world over for their business and technology success. This shows that you do not need to be a 'first mover' to win.

Brin and Page, although they did not invent the idea of search, developed a better search engine by using PageRank, a link rating system which weighted the relevance of web pages. Links that came from relevant sources were given priority over those that did not. For the first time, internet users received search results that were arranged in a logical order and not based simply by matching words in the query with words on web pages.

So the founders of Google had cracked the problem of creating a useful search engine that returned high-quality results swiftly as opposed to a morass of often useless information. PageRank lay at the heart of Google's success.

But however clever a product the Google search application was, it was free to users so it could not pay the bills. So next on the agenda was to find a way to monetize Google. That came again by taking an existing idea, GoTo's pay-per-click advertising, and taking it one giant, leapfrogging step further.

To the right-hand side of the web page, in a new column, and above their 'free' results, Google placed its own version of pay-per-click results, AdWords. In this case, Google mimicked the free search results by ranking ads based on relevance (i.e. their popularity) rather than merely price paid. And Google clearly distinguished with the words 'sponsored links' between the paid-for area and the free.

So Brin and Page created a better product and hit on a way of monetizing it. The irony behind Google's income stream is that it was underpinned by a very long tail of 'old economy' companies anxious to avail themselves of the exposure that the new digital media platform would bring them. Then Google built a global business at warp speed.

The Google founders made two especially brilliant moves which helped underpin that global success. One is the 'Google Story', a relentless PR push portraying Google as the good guys in a bad, bad world (the unspoken villain of the piece is of course Bill Gates, as brilliant as the Google founders, but lacking their charm and apparent innocence). The second was to bring in Eric Schmidt, one of the most experienced technology executives in the USA, as Chairman and CEO in 2001.

There are two important lessons to be learned here. First, far too often companies forget about their 'story' and become bland and amorphous. It was the Google story that helped develop the company's international profile, raising awareness and creating a positive and inviting image around the user experience.

And, second, equally as often, company founders, few of whom are as brilliant as Page and Brin, hang on for too long and are reluctant to bring in professional help when it is needed most. Internet businesses certainly require energy, imagination and brilliance. But they also need seasoned business experience, a subject I will revert to in Chapter Four (The Skills).

eBay and online auctions: internet vs bricks and mortar

Another of the success stories, eBay, similarly recruited Meg Whitman, a hugely talented executive, when the company only had 30 employees. eBay too constructed an 'eBay Story', in this case the famous – but embellished – tale that founder Pierre Omidyar had created the company to help his fiancée trade PEZ dispensers. PEZ is an Austrian sweet that comes in a dispenser which has had many hundreds of different designs over the past 50 years and as such has become a 'collectible'.

Like Google, eBay could not have existed without the internet connecting buyers and sellers creating a perfect market. A very simple idea: a flea market or a car boot sale but on a global scale. Sellers no longer needed expensive retailing space and expensive marketing, and buyers can find what they want quickly. According to a 2005 survey by market research firm AC Nielsen,

724,000 Americans confirmed that their livelihood depended on eBay.

Both Google's 'AdWords' and eBay's auction model reveal another important lesson for internet businesses: don't ignore bricks and mortar. You can have the flashiest technology in the world; but, whatever your internet business, very often it is the smallest, most basic bricks and mortar companies that will underpin your revenues.

One of the big early misconceptions about internet business was that new companies should aim to overwhelm and kill their old economy predecessors. But many of today's internet businesses have built their success by providing access to the internet for old economy, frequently bricks and mortar, companies.

Amazon and e-tailing: delighting the customer

Amazon is different from eBay and Google in several ways. First, founded in 1994, it took longer than those other businesses to reach breakeven, a full seven years from launch. Amazon was written off by many cynics in its early years – I can recall being asked by a professor at a 1999 Harvard Business School seminar whether or not I thought Amazon would ever make money. I, a delighted Amazon customer, answered that it would. (I was asked the same question in 2009, coincidentally also at a Harvard Business School seminar, about Twitter). Second, its founder, Jeff Bezos, remains as CEO. Third, it has a huge old economy component to its cost structure, namely warehouses and inventory.

But just like eBay, Amazon itself has become a highly efficient market place, opening up its platform to third party retailers and making buying easy for consumers. It has excellent execution: solid boxes, shrink wrapping, and reliable, fast delivery. But, above all, its user interface is so superior that other online booksellers, by comparison, are not even out of the starting gate.

Conclusions from the pioneering era

So what conclusions can we draw from these mega-failures and mega-successes?

Don't be put off by the so-called 'dot.com collapse': that is a simplistic overgeneralization which masks the inexorable rise of the internet as a commercial medium. The phrase says as much about investors' lack of due diligence and expertise at the time as it does about the early stumblings of the internet pioneers. Many companies did collapse. But the medium of the internet (and very many internet-based companies) continued to grow.

It is much more evident now which areas of commerce are natural winners on the internet. For example, search is a winner. This explains why Microsoft is so keen for its new Bing engine to succeed against its nemesis Google. In 2009, apparently, there were one *trillion* web addresses and 12 *trillion* free searches.[17] Search is a truly amazing commercial opportunity. On Cheapflights (which I ran for eight years) it allows users to choose from a much wider range of flight options. On Craigslist, it allows them to filter classified adverts to find just what they're looking for. On Match.com, search will even allow you to meet your perfect partner.

Coexistence with the traditional economy is very often a critical success factor. We have seen that Amazon depends on a parcel delivery system for its success. And of course eBay has taken the flea market (a fundamental old economy activity) and positioned it online.

The quick and the dead

Anyone contemplating setting up or joining an internet business will need to appreciate that in order to win you need to adapt and adapt fast. Change is the only certainty about doing business in this environment. Alta Vista, Webvan, Value America did not adapt, Google, Amazon and eBay did, most notably through their increasingly improving technology platforms.

One of the early stars of the British internet firmament was Friends Reunited. A school networking site, it was founded in 2000 and devised a cunning subscription model. Its users were prepared to pay in order to be able to communicate with old school chums. It sold to ITV, a commercial TV company, five years later for £120m.

Two years later, in 2007, ITV's boss, an old media panjandrum par excellence, almost purred with pleasure at his shiny new internet acquisition:

> *Friends Reunited is one of the great undersung (sic) jewels in the crown. It's one of the most important bits of ITV going forward, a massive presence, and it's profitable.*[18]

By 2009, with ITV's television revenues collapsing and its own subscription model long since abandoned, Friends Reunited was sold off for £25m.

Friends Reunited was a very early example of a social network and, to begin with, it was highly successful. But it failed to keep innovating quickly enough and was overtaken by the sudden explosion of the sector with Facebook above all winning market share at a rapid rate.

For entrepreneurs the good news is that the 'dot.com bust' is now history. The internet world is constantly on the prowl for the latest idea – what the author Michael Lewis calls the *new new thing*. Facebook, founded in 2004, is the phenomenon of the moment with valuations running into billions of dollars and global active users exceeding 300 million. In 2009, it also claimed to be cash-flow positive for the first time.[19]

In early 2009, Twitter, founded just three years before, emerged as the newest of these new, new things. It has broken into the top 20 websites worldwide,[20] having shot to fame when it was used as a political tool by Barack Obama in the 2008 Presidential contest and by the opposition alleging fraud in the Iranian election results in 2009. Twitter has no income at the time of writing but its popularity is exploding.

It is too early to say whether either Facebook or Twitter will join Google in the internet's pantheon of long-term successes, and, ultimately, justify their high investor valuations.

The fundamental questions will remain the same for them as for every internet company. Can they maintain their technology edge? Can they monetize as well as simply grow traffic? Can they build a professional management team that is capable of scaling and driving forward the business? And can they do all these things at breakneck speed? In the chapters that follow, I want to give you an idea of how to gain this edge – making sure that you end up with a net profit.

Chapter Two

THE CUSTOMERS – BUSINESS MODELS

There is only one valid definition of business purpose: to create a customer.

Peter Drucker[1]

The word 'customer' is interesting in the context of internet companies. All too often I hear it used very loosely. For some, users and customers are one and the same thing. For example, a user visiting an Amazon website is also an actual or potential customer. And anyone getting a full look at the *Financial Times* website, ft.com, is, by definition, a subscription-paying customer.

By contrast, in many other internet companies, users and customers are quite separate groups of people. For example, Google's customers are the advertisers paying for its AdWords service, not the users coming to its website to search for something. Cheapflights' customers are not the millions of users searching for flight deals, but the flight providers displaying those deals on Cheapflights' websites. TripAdvisor's customers, likewise, are the travel companies who pay to get leads, not the users who scan the content to find hotel reviews.

The purpose of this chapter is to show how internet companies should be clear who their users (traffic) are and who their customers (revenue generators) are, and thus how to establish robust and profitable revenue models. It concludes by emphasizing just how important the loyalty and retention of those customers are.

This is a clear development since the early years of the internet. In the pioneering excitement back then, the distinction between users and customers was not always appreciated. Today, post-dot. com bust, the industry has done some growing up, and attracting users, or traffic, is better understood to be the *prelude* for revenue and profit generation, not the *end game* of your efforts.

On a cold November evening in 2009, I visited the curiously-named Hospital Club, the über-trendy gathering spot of London's digerati founded by Microsoft's co-founder Paul Allen and the Eurythmics' Dave Stewart. The occasion was a seminar on the future of digital media and the keynote speaker was a leading figure in the UK telecom's industry. '*Google*', he declared, was '*the only company making money out of the internet.*' This statement was received with astonishment by the invited guests, who included many veterans of the UK internet industry.

That a business luminary and CEO of a major public company could make such a hopeless blunder betrays much of the ignorance that has clouded the rapidly-expanding digital media industry since the dot.com collapse of 2000. Not only are many companies making money, but it is a most attractive business and one of the few that possesses inherently strong growth characteristics, the recession notwithstanding. This is because internet technology allows you to serve customers better than ever before, across a range of activities, as well as to track customer relationships far more accurately. This chapter will explore some of the best bets for identifying and securing paying customers on the internet, and explain why customer loyalty is a defining characteristic of digital success.

The long tail – providing the leads

When Cheapflights launched in 1996, its publishing platform provided travel companies with something that, at that time, was unavailable anywhere else, not in traditional media nor even at that time on the internet: namely, highly-targeted leads. John Hatt, founder of Cheapflights, grasped the importance of the 'long tail' a decade before journalist Chris Anderson published his bestselling eponymous book on the subject. Hatt worked out that he could serve fliers to Bogota better than any existing media by providing a list of the best prices for flights specifically to that city from the UK. But getting the users was just half of the battle to grow Cheapflights profitably. Hatt needed to acquire paying customers too. From a business perspective, he realized that he was also in an excellent position to sell leads provided from the Cheapflights website, not just to the small number of major brands, but also to a long tail of specialists.

For the first time, smaller travel companies had access to the most targeted leads that their precious advertising money could buy: namely 'intending purchasers' (i.e. users searching with a real intention to buy as opposed to casual browsers) seeking prices for flights to the destinations in which they specialized.

When the movie *Borat* came out there was a sudden upsurge in interest in Borat's 'homeland' Kazakhstan. I took a look at the Cheapflights UK site to see how many clicks were made on the two Kazakhstan destination airports for the year following the movie. I was staggered by the answer: 7,117 clicks on Almaty and Astana.

Put yourself in the position of a travel agency with strong coverage of the Kazakhstan route. Getting access to those 7,000+ clicked searches is highly attractive. Not only that, but you also get to put your prices (and your brand name) up for free, and only pay on results, when a user clicks on the website or telephone link. Can you imagine traditional travel advertising media allowing anything for free? Think about the conversation: you call up the classified advertising department of a newspaper. '*I want to advertise my flights with you*', you say, '*but I will only pay you if you can demonstrate conclusively that they are read by people who are genuinely interested in the destinations which I am displaying. No result, no payment.*' It would be a very short conversation.

Suddenly, in contrast to traditional media, which is far better geared to sell to the big beasts of the travel world, such as Thomas Cook, TUI and British Airways, the smaller players get a chance to compete on equal terms. So from the outset Cheapflights was able to attract advertisers from the very long tail of travel. They could be general travel agents, like Air Tickets Direct of Essex (more of this company later). Or they could be highly specialist companies, like Ocean Florida which specializes in flights (as well as holidays and cruises) to the Sunshine State; Olympic Holidays, which specializes in Greece and Cyprus; and Balkan

Holidays, which specializes in travel to Bulgaria, Croatia, Montenegro, Slovenia, Serbia and Romania.

Now, if you are travelling to Bulgaria and want some information about connections to the historic city of Plovdiv (it is 6,000 years old), you may be able to get it from the agent responding to your enquiry at the big names of travel. Maybe. And on the online travel agency sites you may be able to find some blurb about Plovdiv. Maybe. But at Balkan Holidays, they are set up to deal with queries about Plovdiv. And for Balkan Holidays, the Cheapflights destination pages, covering those six East European countries that they serve – with all those targeted clicks from intending purchasers – are a rich source of potential customers.

This is not at all the same thing as affiliate marketing where you simply sign up with third party sites, have no customer relationships and hope for the best.

Hatt's philosophy was simply to delight his customers. He told them that Cheapflights did not want to lock them into long-term sales contracts. Rather, he would invoice them monthly and if they were not satisfied then they should simply rip up the invoice (apparently no invoice ever was treated in that way). One early customer complained that his monthly subscription was out of line with the leads he was getting. Hatt looked at the number and told that customer that he was right, he would not have to pay and that they should work together to increase the number of leads. The customer was a bit startled, as frequently in British business (sad to relate) the customer is always treated as being wrong.

Taking a long-term approach to customer relations was a lesson I learned on 12 September 2001 in the aftermath of the attack on the Twin Towers. The flights industry was in crisis. Many, not understanding our business, thought that Cheapflights would start to lose clients every which way as a result of the panic. Fortunately for the business, the performance-based model ensured that travel companies were even keener to get the qualified leads than ever.

The one exception was British Airways which was already one of Cheapflights' largest clients and had decided at board level and very publicly to stop all their advertising globally. Alas, our performance-based advertising was, at that time, treated by British Airways' top brass in much the same way as the flowery commercials expanding on the virtues of cabin service and the like (which were of course entirely inappropriate following the terrorists' strike).

My contact in British Airways' digital marketing department called me to deliver the bad news. Of course *he* knew the difference, but there was nothing he could do. He apologized profusely, saying that we should send out the bill in the normal way (British Airways was, at that time, paying a monthly fee) and they would honour it. Beyond 1 October he said he could give no guarantees.

My response was not to grumble about the sudden loss of a key income stream. Instead, I wanted to show our full support for British Airways during this turbulent period. I immediately responded that Cheapflights would *not* charge for the full month (as we were entitled legally to do) but that we would pro rata our invoice to just the first 11 days of the month, the days in which the airline had already received leads from Cheapflights.

The British Airways manager was gracious and appreciative of this gesture; tiny for them of course but symbolic. A few weeks later, British Airways restored all their advertising, and displayed prices once again on Cheapflights' website. The relationship grew and grew to the point where Cheapflights is one of their largest UK providers of online leads[2] and, apart from that one short interruption in September 2001, has been consistently in that position since the airline first displayed prices on the Cheapflights website in 2000.

So the Cheapflights revenue model is based on having broad-based, up-to-date flight price data, and then developing strong relationships with those companies best able to provide data on the more than 100,000 route combinations covered on the UK website alone.

The company has been able to exploit the rapid expansion in airline travel as flying moved from the preserve of the very rich to being a mass market pastime, something which just about everyone can afford. Even Britain's most economically disadvantaged are taking to the skies. According to the *British Attitudes Survey* of 2003, of those who have never worked or are unemployed, a *quarter* fly once or twice a year; and for those in routine and semi-routine occupations, *nearly half* fly once, twice or even three times a year.

And where once almost all flights from the UK were to short-haul destinations, the whole world quickly became accessible. The airlines themselves were a handful of state-owned and monopolistic companies, with some charters and specialists. As a management consultant commuting to Paris in the early 1980s, I can recall British Airways (which was formed as a result of two airlines, BEA and BOAC, being taken into state ownership by the then Labour government of Harold Wilson in 1974) and Air France dividing up the hourly Heathrow slots between them and each charging exactly the same price.

Now there are scores of airlines operating from the UK (scheduled, chartered and the latest phenomenon 'low cost, no frills' airlines). In addition to the airlines, fares are available from many specialists and consolidators. There is also of course a powerful newer group of entrants. These are the 'online travel agencies' (OTAs) of which the best known are Expedia, LastMinute (now owned by Travelocity), Opodo and eBookers (now owned by Orbitz) – all launched within the lifetime of the internet.

So here is an internet revenue model, namely the provision of qualified leads, which really works – using the internet to connect buyers and sellers.

The 1992 movie *Glengarry Glen Ross* is David Mamet's brilliant and utterly compelling account of a rather vile day in the life of an American real estate office. One of the pivotal moments of the film is the address to the sales force by head office honcho Blake (played by Alec Baldwin) who quickly grabs their attention by announcing a sales contest. The first prize is a Cadillac Eldorado; second prize is a set of steak knives; third prize is '*you're fired*'.

He then shows his nervous audience a stack of the much sought-after new leads which, of course, they need. Without the leads: no clients. Good quality leads are much easier to close. And the sales-men have to close to get their commission:

> *These are the new leads. These are the Glengarry leads. And to you, they're gold. And you don't get them. Why? Because to give them to you would be throwing them away. They're for closers.*[3]

Internet leads like those from Cheapflights, Google and eBay are gold to customers. Users who click on Almaty, Kazakhstan, are not there by accident. It is highly probable that they are there, on that page, searching because they *do* want to buy a flight ticket to that destination – the very definition of intending purchaser.

Within the first 15 years of digital media, many of the key 'verticals' (jargon for describing individual industries such as flights or prop-erty or financial services) have been well covered. Sometimes the revenue model is different. For instance, UK property search company RightMove has adopted a subscription model for its advertisers. Other comparison websites charge on a cost-per-acquisition basis (they will get paid when someone actually buys something). The principle is the same across all of them: advertis-ers will pay to be connected with users seeking their particular product. It does not matter if it is domestic electricity, hotels or houses – the vendors will pay for these highly-qualified leads. They are gold.

For websites seeking to monetize effectively, understanding the financial impact of the long tail is really important. This is because it can lead to such a vast customer base. As Chris Anderson men-tions in his book *The Long Tail*, the online DVD rental business

NetFlix offers its customers 55,000 DVDs from which to choose, whereas a typical Blockbuster store may offer 3,000. So if, for example, I am a fan of a specialist genre, say French detective movies, I am more likely to be a customer of NetFlix (or its UK counterpart LoveFilm) than of Blockbuster. Likewise Amazon.com may offer 3.7 million book titles versus a typical Borders bookstore with 100,000 books. If I want to find an obscure biography, where am I most likely to find it?

Winning customers – the traditional economy discovers the internet

Traditional businesses are now playing catch-up as they get to grips with the digital age. No business, however rooted in the old economy, can afford to ignore the potential that the internet brings.

The internet does not necessarily replace 'bricks and mortar' (although it can). More often it is simply a 'wrap-around' which complements and enhances core bricks and mortar businesses.

For every business wanting to extend its customer base, digital media is no longer an option. It is essential. For the traditional economy, it has now become a highly cost-effective, higher-margin sales delivery channel since it requires less infrastructure. That is why, for example, Tesco, the UK's largest supermarket chain, is so keen to drive traffic to its website and why its online supermarket competitor Ocado has been able to raise so much funding. It is cheaper to service customers from warehouses than from expensive stores. Stores need attractive layouts, check-out facilities, security, car parks and the rest. Contrast this to the world in which

Webvan collapsed nearly a decade ago when not only were there fewer internet users but Webvan, a start-up company, was trying to stimulate online supermarket shopping all on its own. Ocado is surely helped by the fact that Tesco – the UK market leader – is itself expanding the online market, as too are Sainsbury's and Walmart-owned ASDA, two of Tesco's biggest competitors.

What the supermarkets have had to do is to create user-friendly websites, ensure that the website pricing is at least the same as in-store, if not cheaper, and, most importantly, ensure that delivery is cheap, regular and with as few substitutions as possible for their shoppers.

The airlines were very early on emphasizing the internet as a sales delivery channel. British Airways has spent years encouraging its passengers to book online. And easyJet was the pioneer of internet booking. Initially, when the airline launched in 1995, booking was by telephone only. All its planes were painted with the telephone number. When asked about the possibility of online sales, Stelios Haji-Ioannou, easyJet's founder, replied that the internet was *'just for geeks'*. It did not take long for him to change his mind. easyJet became the first UK airline to offer online booking in April 1998. Internet tickets were priced more cheaply than those booked over the telephone to encourage easyJet customers to book over the web. Within four years easyJet had sold 10 million seats online.[4]

In March 2009, Ryanair, another major no-frills airline, actually announced the end of check-in desks forcing *all* their passengers to check in online.[5]

Even something as expensive and personalized as scent can be sold online. Take the specialist perfume retailer Ormonde Jayne. Founded by entrepreneur Linda Pilkington, Ormonde Jayne has a single outlet in the Royal Arcade, located in London's most upmarket shopping area, just off Bond Street.

Scent is not something that you can imagine for a nanosecond could sell on the internet since you cannot test it or send it back if not delighted. But in Ormonde Jayne's case, the internet is a huge boon. Her happy clients come from all over the world, as is typical in the luxury goods market, from Tokyo to Dubai to New York. They can reorder their favourite scents, discovered in London, via her well-designed website: a much cheaper, faster and more practical alternative than having to do it all by telephone or mail order, which was a prerequisite in the pre-internet world. The Ormonde Jayne website went live in November 2002. Without using any optimization or other marketing tools to drive sales, in the first year it took £35,000, since when its sales have increased exponentially.

The internet enables Linda Pilkington to neutralize the competitive advantage previously enjoyed by the scent counters of the department stores, which in the pre-digital age would have had the huge advantage of greater customer-handling resources.

But if the digital age is transforming the sales strategies of the old economy – airlines, supermarkets and even upmarket perfumers – what about standalone e-tailers? How do *they* win and retain customers in the digital world?

Winning customers – e-tailers

A colleague of mine recently remarked to me that he buys his shirts now from only one place, an internet company called ShirtsMyWay.com. Their business model is exactly what it says on the tin – selling custom-made men's shirts in millions of different combinations (the company claims over seven trillion, but who's counting?): pockets, collars, cuffs, buttons, buttonholes – all can be combined precisely to your taste. The made-to-order shirts are fabricated by Shanghai-based tailors and then mailed out to you for $65–95 – and the international shipping is thrown in, a nice touch when shipping (disguised as 'postage and packing') is used (abused) as a profit centre by many companies. It takes just 15 days to get your customized shirt using the free shipping option.

I instantly imagined that this must have been a well-funded start-up involving huge amounts of capital. But after a little bit of research I was proved quite wrong. Two entrepreneurs, Peter Crawfurd and Michael Yang, had this idea. They have raised no outside capital. Crawfurd, who has a marketing background, took more than a year to identify the right tailors and fabrics while Yang focused on building the website. Twice he tried to outsource the building, twice he was disappointed. So finally he rebuilt it himself. It launched in February 2009 and by April they were selling 300 shirts per month.[6]

By September they were reporting 1,000 shirts sold. Now that might not sound a lot but even 300 sold per month takes them past their breakeven point. In fact they claimed to be profitable from month one. They spent no money on advertising and focused instead on good search engine optimization public relations and of course word of mouth (which is how I discovered it).[7]

Yang and Crawfurd, both from Denmark, had identified a gap in the market. They worked out that most tailors focus on fit rather than design. By combining both and allowing you to preview the design before ordering it they had established something quite new. It is that visual representation of the shirt online – so purchasers can see it and change it in real time – that is the cunning advantage the entrepreneurs have over the high-street shops (how many shirts can you try on physically in an afternoon?).

Interestingly, you might judge clothing to be a difficult product with which to attract online customers. Shirts are certainly not like flight tickets or books or music. You cannot feel the shirt before buying it. Yet Crawfurd and Yang seem to be onto something. And the men's shirt market is a vast one – over $10bn in the USA alone (2008).[8]

Unlike, say, online supermarkets, ShirtsMyWay is not constrained by geography. So the world is their oyster. And they know very well that shirts are bought not only because they wear out (sadly), and because fashions change constantly (sadly too), but also because men's physiques change as they get older (and that is even sadder). They have probably guessed too that lots of men actually do not enjoy shopping very much and would prefer to handle such matters virtually if they can. So their universe of customers is potentially enormous.

It was an early received wisdom about the internet that it was suitable only for very few sectors: for example, books, CDs and flight tickets – in other words, commodity items that you didn't need to see, feel or try on. For many sectors it was thought that e-tailing simply wouldn't work. When Boo.com collapsed the naysayers argued that clothing, especially high fashion clothing, was just one step too far for the internet.

In fact, clothing is rapidly becoming one of the big success stories of e-tailers. ShirtsMyWay is a promising start-up; and, if you have any doubt at all that a website can prosper by cleverly identifying a customer segment and then serving that segment well, you need look no further than the British clothes e-tailer ASOS.

Coincidentally, ASOS (which is an acronym for As Seen On Screen) was founded in 2000 just as Boo.com was failing. By 2001 it was doing well enough, quietly, to be admitted to the AIM market of the London Stock Exchange (internet success stories were widely ignored at that time as the press preferred to dwell on the disasters). The founder and CEO is Nick Robertson who is the great-grandson of the founder of Austin Reed, a venerable century-old high-street retailer of men's clothing. This contrasted to Boo.com's founders who were rather cruelly thought of as just a model and a poet although, in reality, both had entrepreneurial dot.com experience before launching Boo. Robertson was clearly determined to achieve in the twenty-first century what his antecedent had accomplished in the twentieth: create a major retailing company. In 1999, with £2.4m raised from his brother and wealthy friends in Monaco, Robertson set up an ASOS office in London's Covent Garden.[9]

In less than 10 years, he had achieved that goal: £165m in sales, £14m in profit, with over five million unique users a month.[10] And it ships to 114 countries outside the UK.[11] By the end of 2009, ASOS was reporting a 100% increase in sales over Christmas 2008, making it the UK's second largest online fashion retailer (and the largest purely in e-commerce). Its stock market value stood at over £300m by the end of 2009.

So what has ASOS been doing to achieve this dramatic success in less than 10 years and with no high-street presence whatsoever? It sells affordable replica versions of clothing worn by celebrities. It thus taps into a number of customer priorities: internet shopping (open 24/7); price (especially important in difficult economic times – and how much easier it is to offer good prices without bricks and mortar to worry about); and lastly, one of the biggest trends of the new century, namely celebrity obsession.

The original idea was to sell, online, products associated with celebrities, such as the pestle and mortar used by celebrity chef Jamie Oliver. Then, reportedly, one of Robertson's buyers urged him to start selling clothes to enable people to copy celebrities' looks as well. He started off slowly, with items for sale including black trousers comparable to those worn by Kylie Minogue, and strappy tops worn by the band Atomic Kitten. And the clothes began to outsell everything else.

According to ASOS, of their own label sales, 80% comes from Europe while many high street retailers source their products from China and the Far East. This means that its delivery times are faster. Its ethos is 'fast fashion', from stock to supply – it is quick to interpret catwalk trends and delivery of goods is usually next day. And by manufacturing in Europe the high quality is more easily assured.[12]

A number of activities underpin ASOS's success. These include regular communication with its 1.2 million active customers via email newsletters, which encourage them to revisit the site, and the company's continuous revamping of the website, for example adding new 'departments' such as maternity, launched in 2008, and 'Little ASOS' for kids, which launched in February 2009. This kind of customer relationship is just so much easier, cheaper and faster for e-tailers than it is for their bricks-and-mortar counterparts.[13]

As both ShirtsMyWay and ASOS show, the internet can be extraordinarily disruptive for old economy businesses, especially for operators who have not changed their ways. Sometimes established players are very aggressive. Jamie Murray Wells founded Glasses Direct.co.uk in 2004 (yes, it sells spectacles online) when he was only 21 years old. He wondered why it was that glasses on the UK high street were so very expensive.

So he started a website which sold glasses with lenses at £15 (versus the typical high-street spend on glasses of around £150). Murray Wells describes the opposition from the entrenched industry as a 'witch hunt' with everything from legal letters to hate mail. He says that one of the big opticians even contacted his supplier and threatened to stop buying from that supplier if they continued to supply Glasses Direct. The website had to go down for two weeks while Murray Wells sourced an alternative provider.[14]

Murray Wells's insight was that, with spectacles selling as cheaply as his, they would no longer be an irregular purchase (perhaps bought only on the change of a prescription) but a fashion item which could be worn to suit the occasion – like watches, post-Swatch. The 1991 comedy movie *Soapdish* featured a trendy character played by Robert Downey Junior who changed his glasses in just about every scene. Murray Wells made this Hollywood conceit a practical possibility for everyone. In a way, he is combining ASOS's price-competitive but high-fashion approach (Glasses Direct stocks over 30 ranges of designer frames including Cavalli and Benetton and has just added collections from Vera Wang and Nicole Farhi) with the 'made to order' and price-advantageous approach of ShirtsMyWay.

Knowing that established companies would attack him on the basis of quality, Murray Wells ensures that every order processed by Glasses Direct is reviewed by a licensed optician and is quality checked before dispatch. The antagonistic approach of his old-economy competitors suggests that he has found a good business formula. By 2007 he had sold 150,000 pairs of glasses with a 90–100% growth rate, sufficiently interesting for two of the internet's savviest venture capitalists (VCs), Index Ventures and Highland Capital, to back the company to the tune of a £2.9m investment.[15]

Two years later Murray Wells raised a further £10m in a second round of funding, this time adding German VC powerhouse Acton

Capital to his shareholder group. By this time, he reckoned to have saved purchasers of British spectacles some £40m.

In the first quarter of 2009, despite, or maybe because of, the severe consumer recession in the UK, Glasses Direct enjoyed the most successful period in its history. It remains innovative today, launching a home-trial programme enabling its customers to try on up to four frames at home before they buy. And it continues to develop its online virtual mirror software, which allows users to 'try on' any pair of glasses online.[16]

Given the excitement about social networking and the hyper-growth of internet advertising, it is all too easy to forget about the simplest revenue model of all: making or sourcing something at one price (shirts, fashion clothing, glasses) and then selling it for more. The internet offers opportunities to carry much bigger stock than bricks-and-mortar operations (remember Amazon) and, as importantly, to personalize products much more effectively. Not even the most elegant shirt retailer in London's Jermyn Street can offer seven trillion varieties!

Few products are immune from the power of the internet. A London-based internet business has taken one of the most basic products of all and turned it into a rapidly growing business-to-business opportunity. The internet may be the biggest communications revolution since the invention of the printing press, but what of a business that actually uses the internet to make the *printing press* work better for users! Herr Gutenberg hopefully would have approved of Richard Moross's Moo.com, which takes the humble business card and prints it to order. Its customer base is small businesses, especially those who are keen on design. Several of the internet companies in which I am involved have had their cards made by Moo (which is of course how I know about them – the power of 'word of mouth').

Moo was founded in 2006. Having started with seed capital from the Accelerator Group, it raised £2.75m in that year from Atlas Ventures and Index Ventures. Its first 'signature' product was a tiny but very trendy business card. This 'MiniCard' – the width of a standard business card – but half as high, not only became a must-have among the fashionistas of London's burgeoning design and tech community, but also made business sense for Moo.

According to Moross, these MiniCards, with their new printing process and efficient workflow, optimize his gross margin and make it hard for competitors to replicate Moo's business model. To date, Moo has printed 10 million MiniCards.

Today it makes five different types of card, and by customizing them it takes advantage of the continuing trend towards start-ups and consultants marketing themselves without spending a lot of money on graphic design.

It now ships millions of cards around the world, has over 100,000 customers, grows at 100% a year and has recently opened a produc-tion office in Rhode Island to reduce delivery times and lower costs in the USA, for nearly half its sales come from North America.[17]

Moo focuses on its customer needs very skilfully. Paper selection is naturally a big deal for the company so the entire company apparently gets involved in making the right decision. Moo offers its customers package tracking, advantageous shipping rates and, most importantly, a wide range of product options. You can for instance choose from templates which their designers have created, or upload and use your own image. It offers customers the opportunity to order every single card, sticker or note card in a pack to be different. I cannot imagine walking into a high street print shop and saying '*I want a box of cards but please ensure that each one is different!*'

So Moross took one of the most basic old-economy products of all, the humble business card, and realized that (a) however much we use email, skype, iPhones and Facebook, we still need them, (b) a quality card with great design is an effective way for small companies to market themselves, and (c) via his website he could run his business without the expense of a high street store.

Another successful UK internet business is Moonpig.com. Founded by Nick Jenkins 10 years ago, it provides customized 'build your own' greeting cards. In other words, here is a product ideally suited to the internet, easily deliverable and differentiated from existing bricks and mortar suppliers. Moonpig uses the internet to provide a level of differentiation which traditional high street card shops cannot, just as Moo did versus traditional printers. Like so many successful internet businesses, it is intrinsically viral. People hear about Moonpig when they receive the very original, amusing and professionally-designed cards. My current favourite design shows a man standing over a computer with a sledgehammer bearing the legend:

After several hours of trying to order online, Mr Soskin decided to shut down his computer

You have to be pretty confident about the simplicity of your order process to include that one.

You cannot get individually-designed cards on the high street, not even in the dedicated card shops. Moonpig cards do not cost much more than standard cards and can be printed and posted within 24 hours. For those who think that creating logos requires a lot of money, Moonpig's grinning pig in a space helmet sitting under the moon cost around £200.

A 'niche' business, you might think. Hardly. In his first year, Jenkins sent out some 40,000 cards. Today, reportedly, the number of cards sent out is close to six million. By 2008–09 Moonpig's sales amounted to a healthy £21m with profits of nearly £7m.[18]

Subscriptions and micropayments

One of the biggest internet stories of recent times has been Rupert Murdoch's assault on Google whom he accused of stealing material from his newspapers. Murdoch wants his readers to pay for his content and not enjoy free access. '*Have a delightful, Howard-Hughesian dotage, acting out a crazed, Moby-Dick dumbshow against the Internet*', wrote one angry commentator.[19]

Some newspapers have shown that an online subscription model can work, most notably the *Financial Times* (which has over 100,000 subscribers) and *The Wall Street Journal* (which Murdoch purchased in 2007). Murdoch seems to believe that readers of his other titles (such as *The Times* and *The Sun*) will also be willing to pay in order to be able to access stories online. This seems to ignore the fact that both *The Wall Street Journal* and the *Financial Times* not only attract an extremely affluent readership but also publish very distinct content in a way that the more consumer-orientated newspapers do not. As the director of digital content for Murdoch's rival *The Guardian* bluntly put it, the sort of paywalls Murduch has in mind are '*a stupid idea in that they restrict audiences for largely replicable content. Murdoch no doubt will find this out.*' [20]

Rather than charge a fixed subscription rate (which is rather 'old economy') it might be better for newspapers to charge on a payment-per-article basis. It seems that internet users are increasingly willing to pay small sums for 'must-have' content on an ad hoc basis. Apple's Steve Jobs became the micropayment king when he launched iTunes in 2003 saying '*Consumers don't like to be treated like criminals and artists don't want their valuable work stolen. The iTunes Music Store offers a groundbreaking solution for both.*' [21]

Jobs set the price point for an individual song at 99c. By 2008, iTunes was selling 2.4 billion tracks, with an estimated turnover of $1bn in Q4 of that year alone.[22]

With vastly-improved and secure online payment systems, consumers are now much happier to part with their credit card details than in the early years of the internet, when credit card fraud loomed as a major disincentive to reveal such sensitive information. Jobs has now of course transferred that successful iTunes experience to his iPhone. By the end of 2009, more than 100,000 'apps' were available on the phone, and more than two billion had been downloaded in less than 18 months.

But while Murdoch rails about Google pinching his general news content, others have set about creating websites with unique content and then creating customer loyalty sufficiently strong to be able to charge for that material.

The subscription model certainly suits online dating. One of the earliest internet success stories was that of the online dating sites that remain to this day huge and profitable businesses – perhaps the ultimate way to match buyers and sellers! eHarmony (founded in Pasadena in 2000) reckons that it is responsible for 2% of all marriages in the USA, 236 weddings *a day*![23]

One rival, Dallas-based Match.com (now owned by media mogul Barry Diller's digital conglomerate Inter Active Corporation), claims that its website generates six million dates annually.[24] Match.com (launched in 1995 – another 'survivor') now has sales of $350m a year. In the second quarter of 2009, it had an operating margin of 32%.[25]

Freemium

Jagex is a Cambridge (England)-based producer of online computer games. Jagex's most celebrated game is *RuneScape* which was released in January 2001. *RuneScape* is, in the industry jargon, a Massively Multiplayer Online Role-Playing Game, or 'MMORPG' (pronounced 'em-mor-a-peg').

Part-chatroom, part-adventure game, *RuneScape* explores a vast fantasy landscape that evokes Norse mythology. Players control online characters – avatars – that perform a variety of quests to gain experience or accrue virtual treasure. They fight goblins and explore dungeons but also form complex communities and learn the power of cooperation. The game is never-ending, with new storylines – or quests – added every few weeks.

What *RuneScape* managed to do was displace its more expensive rivals because its players could participate using an ordinary web browser rather than having to buy a CD. It could be played from any computer with an internet connection.[26]

Within one year of its release, *RuneScape* had over one million free accounts registered. The priority for Jagex then became monetization of these customers. It did this by creating a version of the game with extra features that required a monthly fee, while still offering the free version, and by developing partnerships with advertisers. The pay-to-play version of *RuneScape* was released in February 2002, gaining 5,000 subscriptions in the first week, making *RuneScape* one of the largest pay-to-play games in the world. Within five years *RuneScape* had over six million active free accounts and over one million pay-to-play subscribers. *RuneScape*, targeted at teenage boys, was built entirely by word-of-mouth. Jagex received an investment from Insight Venture Partners in October 2005 before which time it was entirely self-funded.

A 27-person operation in 2004, Jagex had around 400 employees by 2008, a year in which it had, reportedly, a turnover of £32m. On this, Jagex made an operating profit of £14.5m, a margin of

45%. Game-time sales accounted for 93% of the business, and that subscription portion is growing more quickly than advertising.[27]

In a 2008 BBC radio interview, then CEO Constant Tedder explained Jagex's success: it had achieved the 'schoolyard buzz'. By being highly accessible to users who would be encouraged to take it up by the free version, *RuneScape* was the activity of choice for male teenagers before they discovered girls and partying.[28]

Music, as Steve Jobs has demonstrated, is an area that is monetizable through micro-payments. Spotify, the music website that allows you to play live just about whatever music you feel like playing (the current choice is six million tracks), has followed the micro-payment model (with a 'buy now' feature). It has allowed limited advertising between tracks as part of its free service and, in a way that is comparable to the *RuneScape* model, you can upgrade to receive music without advertising for £9.99 a month with songs being played at a higher quality as an extra bonus. London-based Spotify (it was founded in Stockholm by Swedes and the development centre remains there) had reached five-and-a-half million users by the summer of 2009 having launched only in October 2008.[29]

Interviewed in September 2009, Spotify CEO and founder Daniel Ek said he thought that subscriptions would turn out to be the majority of his revenues, perhaps 60% against 40% for advertising. *'That's likely because attracting £10 a month from even a minority of users will trump the cheap ad income ... I believe in a freemium model, because information, ultimately, wants to be free.'*[30]

'Freemium', the model used (among others) by Jagex and Spotify – namely offering basic services for free, while charging a premium for advanced or special features – has become very popular.

There are many types of the 'freemium model'. One is the time-limited free trial. Salesforce, the customer relationship management software provider, has used this to great effect, getting potential customers hooked by giving them a full free access trial for 30 days (or longer) and once they've had a chance to sample the full power of the website, converting them to paying users. When a consumer is offered something for free, with no commitment, it's not easy to say no. And if you have a good product, that is the way to get people educated and interested. The mySupermarket online grocery market research product (see below p. 59) also has free registration, albeit for limited access to one brand and category. mySupermarket then offers a free trial for 30 days in which potential customers get to sample the whole system and that is when mySupermarket converts them to paying customers.

Other freemium models include ones that are licence-limited and customer size-based. The idea for the former is to say that for one licence it's free, which will hopefully be enough to get someone within the company interested and using it. It might even provide a perfect solution for small companies. Likewise the customer size-based model offers the service free to companies that are either early stage or with limited revenues. In both cases, even when you give out the service for free, you have the opportunity to win both potential business from those clients when hopefully their company and needs grow, as well as advocates who will tell their friends and colleagues about the service (and as people generally move from job to job more frequently than in the past, there's a good chance that your free user will find themselves in a new job advocating your service). The software industry has adopted this approach, for instance Quickbooks (small business accounting) and Microsoft's BizSpark (support for start-ups), but there is no reason why online businesses should not try it too.

As Danny Rimer, a London-based partner of venture capital firm Index Ventures, points out, the freemium approach works because '*you reduce the main stumbling blocks of product adoption. Web-based users who don't have to pay for it will often start evangelizing the benefits to others.*'[31]

So, as the internet develops into its second decade of customer models, subscriptions (notwithstanding Murdoch's objections to giving stuff away free) do seem to have potential.

Consumers have come to expect the internet to be free for pretty much everything besides retail. However, some websites do manage to make a successful business out of charging for their services. Jagex had an excellent free service. Yet, when it started charging for premium services, people were willing to pay. The *Financial Times* has a thriving subscription service. The conclusion I draw is that if the quality of your product is sufficiently compelling, then you can charge. But if the content is just borderline good, or can be found easily elsewhere, this is a difficult income model to sustain.

Selling the data

Market research has for years been a high-margin business with its traditional staples of surveys and panel data. The vast $70bn US television advertising industry depends on ratings company Nielsen accurately measuring viewers. The internet offers new opportunities to provide accurate, up-to-date and highly-segmented data to customers willing to pay for results based not on limited sample sizes but on the millions of actual users of websites.

An early company to spot the potential of selling data was Australian internet research company Hitwise. Founded in 1997, it launched its competitive intelligence product in 2000. Hitwise pays internet service providers (ISPs) to monitor the daily usage of millions of users. It is then able to segment that data so that you can see on a daily, weekly and monthly basis what market share you have and how it compares with others in your industry. (Hitwise monitors around 1.3 million websites in the UK which are segmented into 17 industry verticals ranging from automotive to travel).

While Hitwise may not be perfect (its data from ISPs means a bias towards home users – it is much harder to track office users hidden behind their security-walled PCs), it nevertheless gives its client a valuable insight into how well websites are doing in terms of market share. It also offers a range of other analytical tools showing, for instance, where your traffic is going to and where it came from (and providing the same data for all the competitors).

As Cheapflights was a very early client of Hitwise, I could see at first hand the power of the data that it was offering. It was important for me to know, for example, for all Cheapflights' key customers what percentage of their website leads we were providing and how we were doing versus other lead providers and advertising platforms. This enabled me to manage the sales effort far more effectively. It also meant that, when we saw our clients, we knew just how important (or not) we were to them as a provider of leads. I could access Hitwise data 24/7, so if I had a sales call on a Monday morning to a particular airline I could research online over the weekend and have an up-to-date picture of our relationship.

Hitwise grew very fast. It used the internet as the means of data generation as well as the channel of data provision to its subscription-paying clients, while their old economy competitors still seemed mired in the age of clipboards, Excel spreadsheets and form-filling. In 2007 it was acquired for $240m by consumer data giant Experian PLC. This demonstrated conclusively the value of yet another potential source of monetization for new media: market research. At the time of its sale, Hitwise had 1,200 clients across numerous sectors including financial services, media, travel and retail.

My own interest in internet data as a means to win and retain customers led to my involvement in two UK companies, both of which provide data, based on site usage and an understanding of its user behaviour. They are in two very different areas: supermarket shoppers, and kids and teens.

mySupermarket.co.uk is a website that compares the prices of supermarket trollies in four of the largest British supermarkets. Now getting nearly one million users a month, the website captures valuable shopping data from a huge range of products and users. This data can be filtered to suit a specific company's needs, and is sold to the supermarkets themselves, to fast moving consumer goods ('FMCG') companies and to financial analysts.

In late 2009, an online version was launched. For a small subscription, you can immediately retrieve pricing data across all four of the supermarkets, going back over a year, for every product and every brand. You can see when promotions took place and chart price changes over time – instant data, available 24/7. The company recently added market share data.

The second is Swapit.co.uk which has a community of kids aged 6–16 swapping goods and earning 'swapits' via its website. 'Swapits' are a virtual currency which can be redeemed for a whole variety of products from playing cards to iPods. By accessing this community, Swapit is able to offer detailed market research to the big kids-facing brands including TV companies, toy and games manufacturers, amusement parks and publishers of books and music.

2009 was not a great year for the big established market research companies. The huge players like the German group GFK and Taylor Nelson Sofres (TNS), now part of WPP, posted poor results. The *Financial Times'* Lex column pointed out that, in the last downturn, providing data and analytics was thought to be defensive. This time around there is something new and that is the internet. '*The internet has no respect for established business models. Market research is counting that to its cost.*'[32]

Selling advertising

In late 1999 I first quizzed Cheapflights' founder John Hatt about his revenue model. Hatt said that his lead-based travel advertising was the core to his business success. Provided Cheapflights could continue to grow, travel companies would continue to pay in ever-increasing amounts for the highly-targeted leads which the website provided. He was much less sanguine about the banner advertising on the website which at the time accounted for perhaps a quarter of his total income. That banner advertising (at that time sold on behalf of Cheapflights by Doubleclick), he said, was an unsustainable revenue stream. And we should not rely on it going forward. It seemed an odd statement and stood in direct contradiction to the online advertising euphoria which characterized late 1999.

At that time, internet advertising was all the rage although, with the benefit of hindsight, much of it was self-feeding. Internet companies raised money from investors and rapidly spent that money on advertising, offline and online. When the money tap was turned off in 2000, so the online advertising market promptly collapsed.

Ten years later, the internet advertising market is once again flourishing but now on a vast scale. UK internet ad spend grew 4.6% to £1.75bn in the first half of 2009 with online advertising expenditure overtaking that of television for the first time.

The UK's Internet Advertising Bureau's figures showed that the internet was now accounting for a record market share of 23.5%. This was the highest for any country in the world, an impressive result for an industry that had not existed 15 years earlier. By contrast, British television had sold its first commercial, for Gibbs SR toothpaste, in 1955, 54 years previously. The figure was all the more impressive because the entire UK advertising sector contracted by 16.6% during the same period.

But anyone launching a business based on advertising alone needs to probe these numbers carefully. For the real driver was search – dominated by Google – which equates to 62.6% of all online advertising expenditure. Total online classified spend accounted for 19.2% of all online advertising spend – and saw a slight decline of 3.6% in this period. Online display was actually down 5.2% year-on-year with an 18.1% share of all online advertising revenues.[33]

In the USA, 2009 was an especially poor year for online advertising, with spending set to drop for the first time since 2002 by 4.6%.[34]

Search advertising actually grew as did video advertising but classifieds, lead generation and banner ads all declined. So search advertising seems to be the most resilient sector, but online display is vulnerable to the vagaries of the general economy. JP Morgan has now predicted a sharp rebound in online advertising supported by a rising economy and actions to reduce the glut of display ad inventory for higher-quality sites and content.[35]

If you want to make money out of online display then you need either to create a vast audience, or to find one that is highly targeted for certain advertisers. Yahoo is a classic example of a large-scale advertiser with a 600 million global audience, lasting the course, when so many of its advertising-based 'portal' rivals fell by the wayside. Yahoo currently has a 13% share of the total US display advertising market and is the market leader.[36]

Acquiring such an audience is in itself very expensive. Just look at YouTube, Facebook and Twitter, all of which have built up huge user numbers, but have been slow to match user numbers with income. According to its founder, Facebook only recently became cash-flow positive despite having some 300 million users.[37]

The other way is to provide niche advertising by offering a compelling user base. Hugh Chappell of TrustedReviews did this when he established his electronic products review website. We will see in Chapter Three how he differentiated his product for users to establish a reader base that eventually exceeded all the relevant magazines put together. He could then provide a highly-targeted advertising model based either on product – so a printer manufacturer can, for example, advertise just around printer content – or on geo-targeting, by allowing advertisers to access users in different countries.

But as display advertising is notoriously cyclical, do not rely on it as your only income stream. It makes sense to consider other sources. Both mySupermarket.co.uk and Swapit.co.uk have added market research. Angie's List, the US website backed by Battery Ventures, which publishes reviews of local businesses and services, derives half its income from advertising and the other half from its monthly fee subscription model.[38]

Customer loyalty

Bain & Co.'s Fred Reichheld has been described by *The Economist* as the '*High Priest of the Loyalty Cult*'.[39]

In 1996, Reichheld wrote a best-selling book called *The Loyalty Effect*.[40] In it, he tested the usefulness of measuring customer satisfaction, used for years as a key performance indicator. You might imagine that high customer satisfaction is a strong indicator for future growth. But, according to Reichheld, you would be wrong.

Astonishingly, he found that there was no correlation between growth and what was then being used as the measure for customer satisfaction. So he then asked himself if 'satisfaction' was being measured correctly. That was when he came across Andy Taylor, the CEO of Enterprise Rent-a-Car, who offered the following insight:

> *The only way to grow a business is to get customers to come back for more and tell their friends.*[41]

In Chapter Three I will describe the importance of product as *the* means to achieve digital success. There is simply no better way to attract users than to have a distinct, 'must-have' digital product. Too many internet companies forget the other side of the business: that is, the paying customer. For e-tailers of course it is the same constituency: for Amazon, as for all e-tailers, the individual customers are the revenue base. But, for digital media companies that rely on advertising in all its online shapes and forms (from lead generation to display advertising), you need to be sure that those paying customers, the advertisers, are happy and, critically, would both become a repeat (i.e. 'loyal') customer *and* recommend the site to other potential customers.

It is understanding how to do this and to be able properly to quantify this that makes Reichheld's research so relevant. As early as 1999, Reichheld realized the relevance of his research for internet companies:

> *In the old world you can have medium loyalty and still make a buck, protected by a convenient location or the customer's lack of information. In the Internet world, there will be no place to hide, no substitute for earning high loyalty. The economics are going to be obvious. People are going to be forced to do the right thing or get out of business.*

> *If you don't earn your customer's trust, you won't make money on the Internet.*[42]

What Reichheld established is that customer satisfaction is quite the wrong measure to use. Looking at many industries, he established that Andy Taylor's *'would recommend to friends'* is the best predictor of growth and profits.

So how do you rate your company's ability to achieve this customer nirvana? Reichheld measured the *'would recommend to friends'* question on a scale of zero to 10, with 10 most likely to recommend, and one least likely. Zero to six he describes as *detractors* who might well be disparaging your product and telling the world that your company is not the sort of place with which people should be doing business. It is the nines and 10s, the *promoters*, who are responsible for all the growth.

The key determinant of success versus failure in customer loyalty is what Reichheld calls the *net promoter score*, that is, the number of promoters less the number of detractors. With this one measure, you have a very practical way of quantifying and managing growth.

When Reichheld did his research, he discovered that across a wide variety of different industries, the median net promoter score was only 11%, quite a contrast to the 80–85% satisfaction scores achieved by the very same companies.

Reichheld's advice was to gather customer data regularly, relating to your customers' perceptions not only of your company, but also of your competitors, and to talk to customers who gave you poor ratings to find the causes.

Reichheld's book was published before the internet had come of age as a business. So his star performers were old economy companies such as Northwestern Mutual Life, Dell, Enterprise Rent-a-Car and Harley Davidson. But just seven years later, it was a new-economy company that Reichheld was describing as having the best loyalty-measurement system in corporate America – eBay:

Their buyer/seller rating mechanism is a loyalty measurement. The idea of open and honest relationships that cannot be manipulated is core to loyalty. eBay's system protects against fraud, against slackers, against anyone who might ruin the feedback system. eBay has software that generates brief email surveys to customers and employees daily. It works in real time.[43]

Fifteen years into its life, the commercial World Wide Web is producing more and more customer segments. Customers can be businesses buying AdWords on Google, or online clients of Amazon (two of the biggest income generators anywhere online or offline). They can be the online subscribers of ft.com or Jagex. They can be consumers buying shirts from ShirtsMyWay, fashion from ASOS, spectacles from Glasses Direct or business cards from Moo. They can be travel companies buying leads from Cheapflights, online companies buying market research from Hitwise, or a myriad of other revenue models – advertising, subscription or e-tailing based. But whatever the model, customer retention is key.

At the heart of customer retention lies customer service, something which was from the outset a core ethos at Cheapflights. It is especially important in the UK travel sector where companies large and small, which congregate at such events as the World Travel Market and the annual Association of British Travel Agents (ABTA) convention, regularly talk to one another. So if you treat customers poorly, word will spread like wildfire and, equally, if you treat them well.

Andrew Nicholson was the founder and managing director of Air Tickets Direct, a travel agency based near Stansted Airport in the

UK, which had a dedicated call centre for offline sales support. Nicholson was an early internet adopter, seeing the huge potential that the web offered his business. One busy day in his offices, which had at that time 13 employees, the entrepreneurial Nicholson was approached by Cheapflights:

> *The company had been to all the big players looking for advertisers and was desperate to find someone. We said 'yes'. We provided 100 destinations and prices to put on the site, and then it was able to go and get other advertisers.*[44]

Helped by the leads that it was getting from Cheapflights, Air Tickets Direct went from strength to strength and by 2001 it had 67 employees. Like all Cheapflights' advertisers, the key to customer service was complete transparency and an open dialogue. It was important then as it is today that the customers were getting value for money. Customer churn, the periodic loss of customers, at Cheapflights has been negligible. Air Tickets Direct remained a customer with Cheapflights and had developed a warm relationship when it was purchased by Travelocity, the American travel giant in August 2001 as part of Travelocity's expansion plans in Europe. The relationship with the small Air Tickets Direct then became part of a much wider relationship with one of the world's largest travel companies, a multi-billion dollar business. Today Travelocity is one of Cheapflights' largest clients and, when Cheapflights decided in 2003 to launch in the USA, the relationship with Travelocity was an integral part of that decision.

Domino's Pizza's billionaire founder Tom Monaghan used to tell his delivery guys to look carefully at the person who answered the door when they called: glance at the person's forehead and imagine that it had $5,000 written on it – not $5 or $10, the price of that particular delivery. Because that is the *lifetime* value of a happy Domino's customer. The same is true of the internet. Customers pay the bills – so take really good care of them.

Whatever business model you choose, the customer is of paramount importance even for virtual businesses that have no bricks and mortar presence. In many ways, without a physical presence, you have to work even harder to delight your paying customers (which, as I have explained, may or may not be the same as your users). The explosion of the internet has seen a similar explosion in business models. This chapter shows just a few of the possibilities that have opened up to entrepreneurs. The stories of successful businesses which I have mentioned in this chapter clearly demonstrate that cornucopia of potential income streams:

- Providing qualified leads (and benefiting from the 'long tail' in so doing)
- Simply using the internet as a wrap-around to benefit a traditional business
- E-tailing – suddenly the world can become your marketplace for everything from shirts to greetings cards (but use the internet to differentiate yourself, not just to mimic the old economy)
- Charging users a subscription *if* you have a compelling reason for people to pay (finding the right girlfriend/boyfriend seems to be one)
- Offering a 'freemium service' where some things are given away (put simply people now expect 'free' on the internet but

can be tempted to pay to upgrade as companies like Jagex and Spotify demonstrate)

- Selling data
- Selling advertising

But, with whatever model you choose to monetize your business, at the heart of success lies customer loyalty and with that customer retention.

Chapter Three

THE PRODUCT

If a man can make a better mouse-trap than his neighbour,
though he builds his house in the woods, the world will make a
beaten path to his door.

Ralph Waldo Emerson (1855)

This chapter will show just how important the user interface (the technology) and the customer offering provided by that interface are to the success of internet companies. It is much easier to be successful as an internet company if you have a radical proposition rather than a 'me too' product – and one that truly delights users so that they will recommend you. You can then build up your traffic without recourse to expensive advertising. These innovative companies are known as 'market driving companies'.

But great and innovative ideas will be nothing unless the user interface works well. Website design is crucial and I offer some tips for success: a poor website can destroy even the best-funded companies: it is important not just to be radical at the outset but to keep innovating: and most importantly you need to protect your intellectual property and defend it fiercely if necessary.

Market-driving companies: radical innovation

In September 1999, at the very height of the internet frenzy, I visited San Francisco. Renting a car at the airport, I drove south to Silicon Valley. Immediately, I was struck by the profusion of garish billboards in every direction proclaiming the wonders of some new website. Why, I asked myself, would new websites, if they were doing something really good and useful for their users, need to spend their money on this? Why were they not investing their billboard money into something with much greater business potential: building a unique product, a product so good that friends and family would recommend it to their friends and family, creating the viral effect that over the years has underpinned the success of so many of the world's leading websites?

For old economy companies, websites are important and will become increasingly so. But as an old economy company (an airline or a shop for example), you can still stay in business without a good website or even without a website at all. At the time of writing there are, remarkably, over one million businesses in the UK who do not have a website, good or bad.

In stark contrast, for a 'pure play' internet business (that is, one that has no offline/'old economy' presence), the website is everything. There is no physical fallback: charming sales people, beautiful displays, subtle lighting or fragrant smells to allure customers. The website is the beginning, middle and, for far too many, the end too. Without a great product, any internet company is doomed from the outset. Spending money on lavish advertising can certainly put off the day of reckoning. But it cannot create user loyalty or a sustainable business.

One important article entitled '*From market driven to market driving*', written in 2000 by three academics,[1] is highly applicable to the digital economy. It explains the 'mousetrap' approach which lies at the heart of digital success. A successful mousetrap will attract users, hopefully getting the world to beat a path to your door.

In order to be a true 'market-driving firm', you need a radical new concept. As described in the article, market-driving firms are generally new entrants into an industry, who gain a more sustainable advantage by delivering a leap in customer value through a unique business system. They create a product/service experience that overwhelms customer expectations and existing alternatives. As a result, the landscape of the industry in which they compete is substantially altered.

Well-known market-driving firms from the old economy include Southwest Airlines, IKEA, Starbucks, Swatch and CNN. You do not have to be the first to market. Southwest was not the first airline nor was IKEA the first furniture retailer. But you do have to bring a radical new concept to the market you are serving.

If someone came to you with a business idea which said 'Forget buying your furniture on the high street. I am going to start a chain of out-of-town stores. You pick up the furniture in bits – branded rather oddly with unpronounceable names such as 'Framsta',

'Barnslig Djur' and 'Forhoja' – in a warehouse. Then, and this is the icing on the cake, you have to assemble it yourself at home with the aid of a manual which may or may not be helpful to you', you would hardly respond 'Brilliant: I want to invest.'

Likewise, if someone had come up to you in the era before low cost airlines and said 'Please invest in my new airline. It will not offer reserved seating. There will be no business or first class. We will not serve food. We will not necessarily fly to major airports', it is unlikely that you would be whipping out your cheque book.

And for sure, if an entrepreneur had once said to you that in the USA the day of the 50 cent watery coffee would soon be over and that Americans would be queuing up for something called a 'Grande Caramel Macchiato' or a 'Venti Mocha Frappuccino® Light Blended Coffee' which would be priced at several dollars, you might have suggested counselling.

But in each of these cases, this was not a business designed by focus groups or endless market research. In every instance, it was the brainchild of one iron-willed entrepreneur. And in each case, the company involved (IKEA, Southwest and Starbucks) has taken its market by storm.

One fascinating observation in the market-driving article was the revelation that all the Swatch watches that sold *best* in the long term were the ones that their consumer market research said would do *worst*.

It is hard for customers and journalists to conceptualize clearly or readily to visualize the benefits of revolutionary products, ideas and technologies. So they require a lot of education. The task facing every innovative digital business which is a genuine market-driving company is to *educate* its customers, users and journalists on the existence of – and how to use – its *radical value proposition.*

As the article revealed, 'market-driving' firms often place greater reliance on the 'buzz network' to get their message across. Because these firms offer a leap in customer value, their customers are only too delighted and eager to notify others about their 'find'. Reporters in trade publications and the consumer-facing press often publicize the radical new innovation. The commitment and enthusiasm of the early adopters and opinion leaders generates excitement – the 'buzz' – and an intangible brand cachet that the market-driving firm strives to maintain. The internet itself enables the buzz effect to take hold more easily. When Cheapflights launched its new meta-search product called Zugu in early 2010, the social networking site Twitter witnessed a crescendo of tweets as opinion leaders tested the new website.

Market-drivers don't find it as necessary to spend a lot of money on traditional advertising; their advertising to sales ratio is often less than that of their established competitors. The very best internet companies have all been market-driving companies. Think, for example, about Google, eBay and Craigslist. Or newer companies like LinkedIn, Facebook and Twitter. Did you learn about them from a TV or radio ad, or see them advertising on a billboard? Of course not: someone told you about them or you read about them somewhere.

Just like their old economy predecessors, they are not necessarily first in the field. Google was not the first search engine but it revolutionized search just as Southwest revolutionized the airline industry.

Now there are lots of ways to drive traffic to websites and that is the subject of Chapter Five. But unless the website has a compelling user proposition, then even thinking about traffic-generating strategies is a waste of time and money.

So the beauty of market-driving companies is that they benefit from the excitement of doing something radically different; they find it easier to win customer loyalty; and of course they spend far less on advertising and promotion.

This is especially true for internet businesses. The reason why Hatt, the founder of Cheapflights, enthused about this academic research on market-driving companies was because he had seen for himself how accurate it was.

Focusing on the product

Of course, Hatt had been clever in all sorts of ways. For example, he acquired great domain names: Cheapflights.co.uk and, later, Cheapflights.com. He purchased the latter in 1998 for the then-staggering sum (for him) of £1,500 – a framed copy of the invoice can be seen on Cheapflights' boardroom wall. He had discovered an unbelievably powerful way of monetizing his website by charging travel companies for the qualified leads he provided to them. But, most importantly, in 1996, he had himself come up with something entirely new on the internet: a publishing platform which allowed British internet users to compare and contrast the price of airline tickets from a broad choice of suppliers.

Cheapflights was launched from his miniscule attic in Eland Road in the London Borough of Wandsworth in October 1996. Coincidentally, this was the same month that another travel website launched – Expedia.

But the differences between these two companies were huge. Expedia was developed by Rich Barton at Microsoft and was funded to the tune of several hundred million dollars. Barton's concept was an online travel agency where, hey presto!, people could buy airline tickets and book hotel rooms via the internet. Barton persuaded Microsoft to invest huge sums in order to enable personal computers to do what in the past only the mainframe airline reservation systems could achieve – retrieve flight information and purchase a ticket. With this investment, Barton and his team created software that allowed users the ability to build customized trips rather than to buy pre-packaged ones, a key innovation that ensured that Expedia was set on a fast track for profitable growth.

In other words, Expedia would replace high street travel agencies with a more convenient alternative (open 24/7) and, in the case of hotels, perhaps a more cost-effective alternative too. Today, Expedia is the largest online travel agency in the world and, incidentally, is an important client of Cheapflights. At the time of writing, it has a $6bn market value.

Hatt's big idea was rather different. Like an online travel agency, an online flight price comparison website was another completely new idea. But there the similarity ended. For Hatt's new business avoided fulfilment. In other words, he did not have to worry about carrying inventory, issuing tickets, taking payments or after-sales service, or financing costly call centres and sales agents. So Hatt could keep his costs very low indeed. But, more importantly, Cheapflights was neutral and independently-owned. It simply sourced flight prices from third party suppliers and then published them on their behalf without any ticket inventory of its own. Cheapflights was thus a publisher, a media company and not an online travel agency. And its impartiality meant that it could genuinely claim the status of 'consumer champion'.

Hatt was a distinguished travel writer. He had for many years been Travel Editor of *Harpers and Queens* Magazine. In 1993, he wrote a book called the *Tropical Traveller, the Essential Guide to Travel in Hot Countries.* He was a veteran global flier, sometimes travelling to very exotic locations.[2]

The problem Hatt repeatedly encountered was how to identify great flight deals. This is a crucial lesson for entrepreneurs. Think about what problems, what chores people face and, what information can be supplied digitally to help them with their daily lives. It is not too late to come up with new ideas. The commercial internet has been around for less than 20 years and the technology is becoming rapidly more powerful.

Back in 1996, British consumers seeking flight deals had few options from which to choose: they could go into their local travel agency or call them on the telephone; they could scour the classified ads which ran for pages in the newspapers ('New York for £199' and the like); or they could look at deals on the Teletext analogue TV service.

Teletext (previously called 'Oracle') was a government-allocated commercial TV information retrieval service developed in the UK in the early 1970s. It offered a range of text-based information, such as news, weather and TV schedules. In 1993, the media behemoth the Daily Mail and General Trust won the monopoly franchise which by this time had soared in value as it was now made available with every single TV sold in the UK. It renamed Oracle 'Teletext' and immediately set about using the system to broadcast flight and holiday deals on behalf of the UK travel industry, which paid dearly to be covered on this popular, and now near universal, service.

Hatt realized that there were problems with each of these options. The travel agencies only offered their own deals which might or might not be competitive. *They* did the searching – so you, as the customer, were reliant on *their* expertise as the agents combed their own systems. As for the newspaper classified ads, they were put together in the sequence that the newspapers wanted. Only big firms such as British Airways and Thomas Cook could afford the prices demanded for the larger ads. Small companies, such as independent high street agencies, could often not afford to appear at all. Content was random and limited. And flight prices were, of course, out of date by the time they

appeared in print. Teletext was painfully slow and offered haphaz-
ard results.

So Hatt thought: what if I can obtain comparative flight prices from
different suppliers (travel agencies, tour operators, airlines – or
'consolidators' who purchase tickets directly from the airlines at
specially negotiated prices) and sort those prices by destination
with a simple index, and publish them on the internet? To get the
full details of the ticket provider, the user could simply 'click' to
get to the provider's website or telephone number. Hatt guessed
that the public would love such a system and that those selling
flight tickets, large and small, would be willing to pay for the qualified leads which he sent to them.

Hatt's first effort at creating the Cheapflights product was quite
basic. He even sourced flight prices from some vendors by fax
because they had no access to email! It was a far cry from today's
sophisticated publishing and meta-search platforms which display
millions of flight prices. But in 1996 it did represent a radical leap
forward. No one else was providing flight price comparison on the
internet – for consumers shopping around Hatt's modest solution
was a quantum leap. A true market-driving idea.

For the first time the consumer could do their searching online 24
hours a day from the convenience of their own home or office
without a travel agent intermediary. For the first time, too, the
consumer could compare and contrast prices across a wide range
of providers on one website which, in contrast to traditional media,
allowed him access to a level playing field. On any city destination

page, for example, a small specialist result would be displayed alongside that of a huge travel company. Initially Hatt used an A–Z index. All a user flying to, say, Bogota, had to do was, first, click on 'B' to bring up all the 'B' destinations. And then a second click on 'Bogota' would take the user to a list of relevant flight prices to that city.

Delighting the user

What sets apart those internet companies that stay the distance and those that don't? The answer is always the same: the product. The internet business is highly competitive and every good idea attracts imitators like bees around a honeypot. Well-financed competition to Cheapflights did arrive very soon after I became CEO.

First off was Stelios Haji-Ioannou (now Sir Stelios), the well-heeled founder of easyJet, who founded a website called easyValue which purported to provide price comparison. It started with a great fanfare and seemed to disappear from view soon afterwards never building the following which its well-covered (and for me scary) press release had presaged. The media magnate Clive (Lord) Hollick (publisher of a leading industry journal *Travel Trade Gazette*) established UTravel. That folded within months.

The hugely successful French internet company Kelkoo (later purchased by Yahoo) launched a travel comparison engine on its website but never made much headway. And Teletext, once a key profit generator for the Daily Mail and General Trust, one of the UK's biggest media companies, never found the same traction on

the web which it had once enjoyed with its monopoly analogue
TV channel.

Web users today are often busy people. Many do not have advanced
technology skills. For them, a 'great website' is one that enables
them to do what they have to do with as little fuss as possible.
Sounds simple maybe, but many internet businesses seem completely clueless about that proposition.

To circumvent any danger of Cheapflights becoming overcomplex, Hatt invented a mythical user called 'Aunt Agatha' and the
'Aunt Agatha test' became a standard benchmark in the company. Aunt Agatha, representing the average non-technical user,
would either find the website easy and helpful to use – or not.
Every new feature or design had to pass the 'Aunt Agatha' test.
All too often, internet companies, founded and conceived by
'techies', fail to appreciate that many of their users actually do not
have enormously developed computer skills, and over-engineer
the product. The result is that too many users are baffled and, in
their frustration, will click away, never to return. Hatt was a talented and popular writer by background, so clarity of presentation
and an appeal to a mass audience was ingrained in his DNA.

Cheapflights has always taken website design very seriously. Ten
'top tips' on website design should have resonance for every consumer-facing website:

1. **Make searching easy.** Searching should be as easy as possible for users, presenting clear user paths labelled with clear
   use of the language.

2.   **Ensure your pages are visually appealing.** Keep them simple and well structured. Being flashy on the internet got old really fast. Enable your users to scan your pages very quickly.

3.   **Give every page a single purpose and focus.** Understand what it is and what you require that page to do, and don't crowd them.

4.   **Optimize your download times.** Users are getting more and more demanding. Websites are getting faster. Users don't like to wait anymore and the likelihood is that they won't!

5.   **Optimize for search engines.** But do this in a smart way that works for the users. Most websites understand the need to create 'search engine-friendly' pages (to attract the traffic that companies like Google, Bing and Yahoo can send them). But don't look spammy – there is no need.

6.   **Spend time thinking through the navigation of the site.** You need to put yourself in the mindset of your user. Also, user test it: ask family and friends if they can complete certain tasks. Remember the 'Aunt Agatha test'.

7.   **Write for the web.** Use short paragraphs and write to the point.

8.   **Make sure your website works in all browsers.** Consider users trying to access it from small screens like iPhones.

9.   **Watch carefully what your users are doing.** Make website changes based on facts, not gut feeling and personal choice! Website analysis is critical.

10. **Place accessibility at the heart of website design.** Take into consideration the visually impaired, users with motor impairments and those with reading difficulties.

I would add an eleventh rule: **Make the home page as simple as possible**. Never *ever* present a home page with a tiresome overcomplex design involving animation with the legend 'skip the intro'. If you can 'skip the intro', you should abandon it altogether.

Relentless focus on getting the website right is common to all successful internet companies. Take the UK's TrustedReviews.com which, by 2008, was the UK's most visited website in the category 'computers and electronics'.[3] It is quite an achievement to obtain more traffic than major household names such as Canon and Panasonic. I asked its founder, entrepreneur Hugh Chappell, why TrustedReviews has achieved such a vast following. He gave a simple answer:

For me, it was all about the product!

The TrustedReviews idea had been conceived only five years before in 2003. Sales of computer magazines had been melting away for years. Why? With the passage of time, their readers were technically more aware and so they bought fewer magazines each month. More importantly, however, the internet itself was fast becoming the established medium for information.

The challenge that Chappell faced was to provide a better product (for both his users and his advertisers) than either magazines or indeed magazines with websites. It is worth looking at the various actions taken by Chappell to get his product right.

He published content instantly rather than (in the case of magazines) once per month. This was particularly important for news as well as reviews of the latest and hottest products. He produced an online-only version to avoid conflict with a print version. Print publishers tried both, constraining their website in order to avoid cannibalizing their magazines.

He hired professional journalists from the magazines; so there was no argument in terms of quality of content or credibility. He provided quantity as well as quality. TrustedReviews.com published three reviews per day, seven days per week, in addition to many news articles per day. His website had more detailed reviews than the magazines as they would limit their content to a single page or less. Paper costs publishers money! He separated content into individual sections to enable readers to find relevant content quickly.

He provided only original content (written and owned by TrustedReviews Ltd) which could not be read elsewhere. He offered his users access to all content, i.e. thousands of reviews, as opposed to just tens in a single copy of a magazine. And he made access free for users: no charge to read content on TrustedReviews. This compared with an annual subscription to a computer magazine of typically £40.

TrustedReviews, just like Cheapflights, kept its design very simple – a home page with the very latest news and reviews updated many times per day (seven days per week), and sections for each category, for example camcorders, printers and laptops.

In Chappell's words:

> *User delight ultimately came from writing excellent content in a style/tone relevant to our core audience. TrustedReviews.com is a relaxing*

read. Most importantly, users are very happy to buy products recommended by the publication.

But, however good the product, no internet company can ever sit back on its laurels. Paranoia is a prerequisite for successful internet companies. For internet companies, the speed of innovation is breathtaking. Alta Vista collapsed because it did not innovate its search technology quickly enough. In the UK, Friends Reunited, once one of the country's most popular websites, did not respond quickly enough to the new generation of 'Web 2.0' social media competitors, above all Facebook. 'Web 2.0' is the term coined for the second generation of internet sites. But the truth is that the internet sites have been developing quickly since 1994.[4]

Both Alta Vista and Friends Reunited were pioneers but they did not keep up the pace.

Every successful internet company has one defining characteristic. It has a great product which users will enthuse about and come back to time and time again. That was why Google triumphed where other search engines failed and why Facebook has become so universally popular. Clearly, however good the Facebook idea was, it needed to develop an interface which worked not just for the technology cognoscenti but quite literally for everyone. It succeeded. By 2009, total minutes spent on Facebook in the USA alone had increased by nearly 700% year-over-year, growing from 1.7 billion per month to 13.9 billion.[5] In the UK that *monthly* figure was 3.8 billion minutes – or an hour spent on Facebook for every man, woman and child in the country.[6]

Uncluttered pages. Clear navigation. Attractive design. It all sounds so simple. In reality, the temptation to provide cluttered web pages and the financial demands of monetizing such pages often render websites muddled and incoherent to their users.

The peril of poor websites

Designing a great website is not necessarily just a matter of spending money. Famously, London-based Boo.com, an online clothes retailer, spent millions building its website. In 2001, a year after its demise, its Swedish co-founder Ernst Malmstem bravely wrote an account of its collapse.

He described the usual farrago of cost overruns, endless money-raising rounds and legions of expensive employees occupying volumes of prestigious office space. But the book is curiously short on detail about the website. Revealingly, Malmstem actually uses the term 'hyper-growth' to refer to his *payroll* rather than user numbers or income.

The website never seems to be the core of Malmsten's concern. Talking of his designers located on the top floor, he says:

> *On my way past the office after late dinners in Soho, I would look up and almost always see the lights burning on the top floor. I tried to make it up there a couple of times each day to see how things were going and to keep people motivated.*[7]

He makes it sound like a distraction rather than a central part of the CEO's job. No internet CEO can afford to ignore the product.

It has to be a fixation where no detail is too small and where second-best has no place.

One of the world's leading internet design experts, Jakob Nielsen, described the Boo website in late 1999 as 'clumsy', 'slow', 'unpleasant' and 'not nice'.[8]

We are told by Boo's co-founder that, just before his website was scheduled to launch, he brought in an e-consultancy called Viant to review progress. It seemed that Boo's content management system (the driver of what appears on the website) was a bit faulty. Actually it was more than a bit faulty. One concerned Boo employee told his boss that Boo's customers would not be able to buy anything or would receive the wrong items in the post.

This provoked an earthy reaction from the top man:

> *I was shaken. This was the nightmare scenario. It would have been better to have been found in Hyde Park with a prostitute.*[9]

The consultants' findings were not encouraging:

> *Our site was cluttered and hard to use. While the user interface achieved a high cool factor, there was nothing yet in place to create an indispensable site for Boo's target audience.*[10]

There seems to be quite a strong correlation between internet companies that fail and those where product simply does not have supremacy. Another example is govWorks.com which was immortalized in the 2001 film documentary *Start.up.com*. This should be required viewing for all internet entrepreneurs. Using a 'fly on the wall' documentary technique, the movie charts the course of co-founders Kaleil Isaza Tuzman and Tom Herman from 1999 during the euphoria of govWorks' early days to 2000 when the company finally burned through the last of its $60m of investors' cash.

Again, govWorks spent a lot of money on its website. But seemingly to no avail – it was full of glitches. The glaring inadequacy of its search functionality is laid bare in the movie. Towards the end of the film, the hyperactive and energized Tuzman, a former Goldman Sachs banker, admits *'Our site is not as good as our competitor's site.'* In the internet business, that is almost like saying *'Game over: we are dead.'*

Innovate

Cheapflights' founder Hatt often says, *'there are only two sorts of internet company: the quick and the dead'*. Not only did he found a company with a completely original idea, he also imbued it with the ethos of constant innovation. So, for example, Cheapflights, the inventor of flight price comparison, was very prompt in launching a 'multi-booking engine'. This compared, in real time, results from several flight providers (a simple idea now copied by many). We also, very early on in the history of the internet, compiled a list of 'opt-in' newsletter subscribers and sent them targeted emails. We published one of the first travel blogs (*Cheapflights News*) which brings users up-to-the-minute news about flights.

Why did Amazon succeed where so many early entrants into online retailing failed? Quite simply, it understood about the primacy of the website and the imperative of constant innovation. Amazon has always enjoyed spectacularly clear navigation and an easy ordering process. It clearly listens to its users very carefully. Its site modifications are insightful and make sense. All too often websites overhaul themselves by adding bells and whistles, which are in fact counterproductive, making them harder and harder to use.

In recent years, Amazon has led the way in the new direction of 'personalization'. By observing user behaviour, Amazon can identify its users' interests and make informed and useful recommendations based upon them. My home page says '*Hello David Soskin*' (my local chain bookshop never welcomes me by name) and offers me '*David's Amazon.co.uk*' which contains pages of suggestions of books and music to buy now or coming soon. And there I find novels by Patricia Cornwell and Philip Kerr, two crime writers, as well as music by Led Zeppelin and David Bowie – all relevant and useful to me.

As Jeff Bezos says: '*My view is there's no bad time to innovate. You should be doing it when times are good and when times are tough – and you want to be doing it around things that your customers care about. For us, it's such a deep-seated belief, I'm not sure we have a choice.*'[11]

Today Amazon continues to innovate. Remaining true to its roots as the world's most effective online retailer, it has extended its reach from its original book franchise to a myriad of other products. Most revolutionary of all perhaps is the Kindle, its electronic book reader which takes Amazon into a new world, that of consumer electronics. It is difficult to imagine an 'old economy' company prepared to take that sort of risk.[12]

Another company that has found an interface that really delights its users is Craigslist. Just look at Craigslist's popularity: over 20 billion page views per month, putting it in 30th place overall among websites worldwide; eighth place overall among websites in the USA; over 50 million unique monthly visitors in the USA alone. With over 40 million new classified advertisements each month, Craigslist is the leading American classifieds service in any medium. For instance, it receives over one million new job listings each month, making it one of the top job boards in the world.

No wonder that, in the USA, traditional newspaper classified advertising income has dropped from $20bn in 2000 to $10bn today – a halving in under 10 years. The number of adults in the USA who have used online classified ads has more than doubled in the past four years. Almost half of American internet users now say they have used online classified sites, compared with 22% in 2005.[13]

Craigslist's design is counterintuitive as it has shunned visual appeal in favour of sheer usability. Their users want simplicity and they get it. Jim Buckmaster, CEO, explains why the company has rejected elaborate design:

> *Our very modest approach works for end users...for an individual user their ad can be as flashy as they like but the top level pages load*

faster if they're simple, blind people are able to access our site, it doesn't get in people's way.[14]

Keeping the product simple has been at the heart of Craigslist's success. Rejecting both banners and a click-through model, it breaks every internet rule as its website looks old-fashioned and a bit clunky. But, much more importantly, it works and works well. The innovation here is the use of the internet to provide listing services – in Craigslist's case general classified ads. Others, such as Monster.com in jobs and Zillow and Trulia in property, have also used the internet to great effect to disrupt traditional media revenue sources.

Other examples of websites working well for their users are those of British Airways (a calendar showing which day offers the cheapest flight price was a neat addition and has since been imitated the world over); NetFlix and LoveFilm, each of which strikes a brilliant balance between suggesting movies based on previous orders and crystal-clear search functionality; and the BBC, which has excellent navigation and super-fast downloads.

When innovating, one of the great advantages of the internet is that you can make changes to websites and test those changes quickly, cheaply and easily. Analysing user 'metrics' (that is, ways of following what users are doing on websites) is now so sophisticated that you can rapidly spot what will work and what will not. Different types of websites will have different metrics which are important. Unique users, visits, repeat users, clicks per page, time spent on the website are all examples of measurements which can calibrate the progress of your website.

You have to keep trying. And never be afraid of doing the wrong thing. Often websites can go live in 'beta' (which is supposed to be the test phase) for years. As IKEA's founder Ingvar Kamprad said:

Only while sleeping does one make no mistakes. The fear of making mistakes is the root of bureaucracy and the enemy of evolution.[15]

That may explain why so few good internet ideas stem from major companies. Rich Barton developed Expedia while at Microsoft: so all credit to Bill Gates for backing him. But how many other internet successes have been incubated in mega-corps? One reason is that big companies have a culture of 'sticking to the knitting' (and in the case of traditional media this is somewhat surprising as the knitting is disappearing rather quickly). But another reason is that many who work in big companies have an inherent fear of failure and this makes them highly risk averse. Not the optimal characteristic for inventing a new internet idea.

Because of the 'viral' word-of-mouth characteristic of the internet, clever and original websites catch on like wildfire. Spotify, the European music site, reached five million users within a year. Perhaps Facebook, with its 700,000 new members *daily*, and its global reach is the classic example. More recently Twitter – with its easy-to-use micro-blogging platform – has enjoyed global adoption too. Because of the increasing reach of the internet, and the decline in technology costs, the opportunities for small start-ups to grow and then to go global are perhaps greater than in any other form of commerce in history. But innovation is key.

Protect your intellectual property

There is absolutely no point in getting the product right and then failing to secure the intellectual property ('IP') rights to it. Without protecting the IP, success is likely to be short-lived.

Amazon has been a vigorous defender of its own patented technologies. For instance, it has defended its patented 'one-click' purchasing technology, suing barnesandnoble.com in October 1999, claiming that its technology had been copied. (The suit was settled in March 2002, but the terms were kept confidential.)[16]

Facebook's early history was mired in IP controversy. The owners of another social networking website called HarvardConnection (changing its name to ConnectU in September 2004) filed a lawsuit against Facebook's founder Mark Zuckerberg. They claimed that he had: broken an oral contract for them to build the Facebook site; copied their idea; and illegally used source code which belonged to them. The parties reached a confidential settlement agreement in February 2008.[17]

ConnectU filed another lawsuit in March 2008 attempting to rescind the settlement, claiming that, in negotiations, Facebook had overstated the value of the shares in the business which it was granting to the ConnectU founders as part of the settlement. In February 2009, it was reported that another settlement had been reached between Facebook and the ConnectU litigants with Facebook paying $65m to the plaintiffs, most of it in Facebook shares, and $20m in cash.[18] This quagmire of legal action demonstrates that, if you have a good or original product, be sure that it is robustly protected.

Bricklin's pioneering of the financial spreadsheet provides another salutary tale, which is related in his book *Bricklin on Technology*.[19] The spreadsheet was one of the great inventions of the twentieth century. And it revolutionized the use of the personal computer. But Dan's patent attorney told him at the time that it was very unlikely that he could obtain a US patent for his invention. For, in 1979 when Visicalc was introduced it was very unusual for patents for software inventions to be granted.

It was not until 1981 that a US Supreme Court decision opened the floodgates for software patents. As Dan writes: '*Unfortunately for the players in the Visicalc story, the decision came too late to help us patent the spreadsheet.*' Dan was not alone. Cut and paste, the word processing ruler and hypertext linking were all technology innovations that were not patented.[20]

TrustedReviews' founder Hugh Chappell says: '*Intellectual property rights are the most important assets many businesses possess.*' He tells the cautionary tale of a website that he was looking at buying, only to discover that its primary domain name was registered to the girlfriend of the man who owned the company! '*Picture the scene five years later when a multi-million pound offer is made to buy the business, with one slight problem – a jilted, upset and now former girlfriend still owns this key asset.*'

So if you think you have the next big internet idea, proceed with care. Remember that ASPIRIN, ESCALATOR, CELLOPHANE, LAUNDROMAT, THERMOS, TRAMPOLINE and VIDEO-TAPE were all originally legally-protected trade marks. But, in each case, the legal protection in due course became invalidated. Why? Because its owner had been unable to prevent the mark from being used as a generic word. The unhappy result (for the owners) is that all these words have now passed into the ordinary vocabulary and the legal protection that they once enjoyed has, to a greater or lesser extent, been lost.

Even something as simple as a domain name needs careful protection. For example, to guard against 'typo-squatting', it is often a very good idea to include misspellings in one's portfolio of domain name registrations. You do not want to take the risk that your competitors get hold of domain names that are too close to yours for comfort. It can be worth going to some lengths to do this. In a 2004 case the no-frills airline easyJet had to go to the World Intellectual Property Organization's Arbitration and Mediation Centre in order to recover ownership of the domain name www.easyejt.com (sic).

To underpin a claim to a domain name it helps to have evidence of prior trade mark rights to the name. For example, in a 2007 case involving a dispute over the ownership of the domain name www.webtv.eu, the claimant failed to secure ownership of it. This was because, although he was able to demonstrate that he owned an EU Community registered design including the words 'web tv', he could not show that he owned any *registered trade mark* rights in the word.

The other side of the coin is that you have to be careful when using material from the internet in your business. For instance, do not imagine for a moment that you can download any images from the internet without having to pay for them. For example, it was reported in late 2009 that a removal firm called JA Coles was obliged to pay damages and legal costs to Getty Images for having used, without permission, a single image (taken from the internet) of a mother and daughter smiling at each other.

Like all pioneer territory, law is being made as the digital industry progresses – a hazard for innovators who are actually driving new laws as well as products. Google 'AdWords', the pay-per-click advertising platform that Google offers to paying clients, has proved a legal minefield. For example, at the end of 2008, Interflora Inc. sued Marks & Spencer for trade mark infringement because the British retailer had bid for the words INTERFLORA and INTAFLORA on Google AdWords without Interflora's permission.

Finally, for those who need some guidance as to the do's and don't's of IP, the London law firm of Wedlake Bell provides a handy checklist:

DO	**DON'T**
…carry out research into whether your proposed brand might infringe third party intellectual property rights (IPRs) before deciding on it	…disclose (other than in confidential circumstances) any patentable invention until after you have filed an application to patent it

DO	DON'T
...select, as your brands, words that are (so far as possible) distinctive and non-descriptive	...use (or allow other people to use) your trade marks as generic words
...apply as soon as possible to register your business name and key brands as trade marks	...use 'invention promotion' agencies without exercising caution
...apply as soon as possible to register your business name and key brands (and 'lookalikes') as domain names	...place the symbol ® adjacent to your trade mark unless the trade mark has been registered
...keep ongoing evidence of your brands' goodwill and reputation, and your investment in them, so that you can if necessary use them as evidence in passing-off actions	...commission any consultant or external agency to create any copyright works for you without obliging them in writing to assign the copyright to you
...apply as soon as possible to register new and individual product designs that you develop as registered designs	...threaten infringement action against anyone without being sure that your threats are justified
...monitor the market constantly for third party products or services that might infringe your IPRs	...use any third party brand as an AdWord or other keyword without having taken professional advice
...use DIY methods to record the creation and ownership of copyright works like (for example) software	...extol your products and services by comparison with your competitors' brands without extreme caution
...deter potential infringers by marking your works with (where appropriate) the symbols © and ™	...forget to renew your registered trade marks and domain name registrations

DO	DON'T
...make full use of publicly-available IP information services provided by institutions like the Intellectual Property Office, the British Library and the Design Council	...allow anyone else to make use of any IPR without them having signed a properly drafted licence

© Wedlake Bell 2009, J.P. Cornthwaite author.

For internet entrepreneurs, four basic lessons emerge from this chapter:

- Come up with a radically different idea (that is become a market-driving company)
- Make sure that your user interface truly delights
- Innovate constantly and do not be afraid of experimenting
- Protect your intellectual property.

Chapter Four

THE SKILLS

The way a team plays as a whole determines its success. You may have the greatest bunch of individual stars in the world, but if they don't play together, the club won't be worth a dime.
Babe Ruth – American baseball player

The story of the internet has been so much about technology that the 'people side' often gets overlooked. Yet people are crucial. This is a brain business, and internet companies depend on the creativity and skills of their teams. It is imperative to attract stellar talent and then to keep it. This chapter looks at the role of the CEO and how to get recruiting right. It outlines some ideas to help motivate and retain people. It emphasizes the importance of location and office space. It considers outsourcing, professional advisers and the crucial role of boards.

Leadership: but you may have to buy the milk

Leadership is vital to harness all the potential in the team. So what does leadership entail? Just as for the CEO role in any business, it is absolutely necessary to inspire and motivate the whole team with a clear message and a strategic vision, and to show determination and the will to win. Beyond this, a CEO needs business acumen and operational expertise. So it is a combination of the talent necessary to run the business, the right attitude to prevail over the competitors and the motivational skills to take the team along the journey. One venture capitalist recently told me that, when considering potential CEOs, he looks for the '*healthy instincts of a born winner*', a nicely Darwinian description.

It is easy to assume that, to run a successful internet company, you need to have a technology background. Google's Eric Schmidt has technology degrees from Princeton and Berkeley. Amazon's Jeff Bezos, likewise a graduate of Princeton, has a degree in Computer Science and Engineering. It is noticeable how many successful internet entrepreneurs do have technology backgrounds (Evan Williams of Twitter and Mark Zuckerberg of Facebook being two further examples). However, Meg Whitman, yet another Princeton graduate, who built eBay from a 30-person early-stage business into an international corporation, took her degree in Economics with a subsequent MBA from Harvard. The conclusion I draw from this is that intelligence is an obvious necessity; but although helpful, a technology background is not absolutely essential.

In any start-up or early-stage business, a CEO needs to be particularly hands-on. This is especially true in the digital economy as it moves ahead at great speed. Any CEO remote from day-to-day activities will soon be overwhelmed by the shock of the new. In the bricks and mortar economy, there are more established ways of doing things. Internet CEOs are still today pioneers of their craft. The only rule is that there are no rules. Because it is a brains business and the skill base matters so much, CEOs need to manage their workforces of often young and relatively inexperienced talent carefully, and to adapt their teams to the ever-changing business requirements – including rapid hiring and occasionally firing.

Cheapflights is now an international business operating websites in half a dozen countries. It was not always like this. When I started back in early 2000, the company had precisely three employees (including me). We sat in a small serviced office above Foxtons estate agents in Wandsworth, South London. We had a guy with travel sales experience – so he managed our customers. My business partner Hugo came from a property and entrepreneurial background. I was most recently a media banker. Initially we divvied up the tasks between us and avoided job titles.

Eventually we required a little more structure and I became CEO. In this role strategic vision, raw business acumen and operational skills were basic essentials. But someone had to bank the cheques, do the photo-copying and buy the milk. In those early years at Cheapflights, I had to make sales calls, answer user feedback, and decide what banner advertising was appropriate for the website. I even managed our 'pay-per-click' marketing campaigns. It was a very useful apprenticeship.

Apart from programming, there were very few activities in the business in which I did not get directly involved. This experience was to prove invaluable when later I came to recruit for the company.

Recruiting

Internet commerce is not for the faint-hearted. It requires extraordinary dedication to succeed. Developments on the internet move at enormous speed; the barriers to entry are minimal; it is global; and the loyalty of users is under continual threat. In short, it is not a safe haven. Working in an internet company is like playing squash blindfolded. You never know from where the next high-velocity shot is going to come.

Recruiting talent is one of the most difficult and important roles for any CEO. This is especially hard in an early-stage company when funds are not plentiful, premises are not glamorous, and teams are either tiny or non-existent. It is tempting to aim low, but I once heard some sage advice from a Harvard Business School professor:

Hire not for where you are now but for where you want to be.

He told the inspirational tale of a tiny company, with just $1.5m of investment, that had developed a very cheap electric tooth-brush called 'SpinBrush'®. The company positioned SpinBrush® not as a cheap substitute for expensive electric toothbrushes but rather as an affordable and more effective substitute for the traditional manual ones. Priced at just $1 more than the most expensive manual brushes, the company reckoned that many consumers would trade up. They spent 18 months designing and sourcing a high-quality brush that wouldn't cost more than $5, batteries included. '*If it had cost $7.99, we wouldn't have gone forward*', the founder later said.

The company's masterstroke was not to hire some cheap and cheerful sales guy with their limited budget. Instead they pushed out the boat and hired a very experienced top salesman, namely

Joseph A. O'Connor from Clorox, a multi-billion-dollar food and chemical company. It was an inspired choice. O'Connor, who had years of experience selling to Walmart and other big chains, persuaded a health and beauty-aid manager at a Phoenix Walmart to buy 240 SpinBrushes®. '*They sold out over the weekend*', he recalled.

In 2000, the company, two years after it was started, sold 10 million SpinBrush® units, more than trebling the existing US electric toothbrush market. And in another two years, Procter and Gamble acquired SpinBrush® for $475m.[1]

So a $1.5m investment led to a $475m payout.

The lesson for early-stage companies is clear: hire the very best people you can, even if it means stretching resources. At Cheapflights one of the first people we recruited was the finance director. We had started with a part-time bookkeeper; but it became clear this was insufficient to support the rapidly-growing business. So we set about finding our first full-time finance person. Initially, given our minute budget, we were looking for someone relatively junior who would grow with the job. We interviewed many young hopefuls; but they all proved a bit underwhelming.

By pure happenstance, I mentioned the frustrating search to a friend, a successful Northamptonshire surgeon. He said that a near neighbour was an experienced finance executive looking for a new role and that I should talk to him. And so I did. The candidate was far more experienced – and far more expensive – than the job brief had allowed for. And hiring someone of his experience in a company that was turning over around £1m per annum was overkill. But I could see that Cheapflights was going to continue to grow very fast and had observed the chaotic finances of so many dot.coms. I realized that here was someone who would immediately impose an iron grip on the company's finances and provide clarity to reporting, which is so important in a hyper-growth environment. It was a classic case of hiring for 'where we wanted to be'.

Not that we always got it right in the early years. The rapid growth of the company, at a rate of 50% per annum, combined with the harsh competitive dynamics of the internet business, meant that some colleagues just burned out. Others could not grow professionally fast enough to keep up. But, despite this, many of those early recruits are still with the company today, nearly a decade later: our head of international, two of our leading UK commercial team members, as well as the finance director, all date from that early period in Wandsworth.

One disadvantage of those early years was that the pool of people with real internet experience was miniscule. In the late 1990s internet commerce was by and large rather amateur. Everyone was learning on the job. And it was full of people who thought it was easy money. Now of course 'résumés' can display genuine depth of relevant experience. So digital businesses can hire with greater confidence. But do check and recheck those résumés. In two cases, I have come across people who have simply lied about their qualifications.

One of the hardest recruiting efforts at Cheapflights has been for the top technology slot. As is typical with many internet companies, the demands grow exponentially, and what is suitable at a very early stage can become less suitable as the company changes. One early chief technology officer (CTO) did not show enthusiasm at the thought of building an international platform. A super 'early-stage' guy, he helped hugely to improve Cheapflights' first publishing efforts. But then came our decision to expand into the USA and he decided that he did not want to take on this immense task. Putting it bluntly to me, he said he could not contemplate building a database for a country with quite so many departure airports (the UK at that time had about 30). We agreed together amicably that it was time for him to move on.

The CTO at Cheapflights who did finally build our international platform had spent years at IBM. But he combined that with more recent experience of a lean, mean successful e-tailer which had given him a taste for (and experience in) the smaller company environment. In 2008 his achievements at Cheapflights were recognized when he was named in the UK's top 10 CTOs in the 'Retail & Leisure' sector by Silicon.com, a leading UK technology and business publication.

Apart from hiring with the future shape and size of the business in mind, when assembling a senior team, there are other important elements of recruiting to 'get it right': the use of search firms, rigorous interviewing, cultural fit and, for senior roles, 'psychometric' testing. Psychometrics is the branch of psychology which deals with the testing of traits such as intelligence and aptitude.

Using headhunters is extremely expensive and early-stage companies will want to do everything they can to avoid using them, preferring instead personal networks. But they can be useful for three main reasons. First, quality candidates will take telephone calls from the better-known ones (which they might well not do from the company directly). Second, the reach of the headhunters is extensive, and as the internet is a global business, good candidates are by their nature global. Third, search firms relieve the company of much of the time-consuming organizational burden of arranging rounds of interviews and vetting résumés. A good headhunter will spend a lot of time with the company to understand its needs. This is a prerequisite for a shortlist of excellent and well-matched potential candidates. And their objectivity can be helpful when trying to crystallize a job specification.

I have used many headhunters over the years, from the world's largest and most prestigious firms to the smaller boutiques. Price is one consideration and it is certainly worth shopping around. But the most important factor is their track record: whom have they placed before in the digital economy, and on whose behalf?

Personality also matters. A rather pompous and patronizing partner at one well-known firm of headhunters in London made the mistake of keeping his feet on his desk when talking to one of my senior colleagues. As a consequence the firm has never had any business from Cheapflights. The idea that potential candidates would be grilled by this individual, whose personality was so alien to the Cheapflights culture, was too terrible to contemplate.

At the other end of the spectrum is a headhunter we have used with enormous success in Boston. Thoughtful and experienced, he has immersed himself in our 'corporate values'. He is well wired into the whole Massachusetts technology scene so he has a good grasp not only of the talent available but precisely where everyone is in their careers.

Another ingredient of successful recruitment is, first, to involve as many people in the company as reasonably possible, a technique which I had learned at Bain & Co. This minimizes the chances of making mistakes (there is no such thing as error-free recruiting). Second, it helps achieve a consistency of corporate culture which underpins successful performance. And third, it is empowering for colleagues to get involved in adding to the team rather than having individuals imposed upon them.

Often new employees would tell me afterwards that they were surprised just how long the recruiting process took. I would then explain how dreadful and time-consuming the consequences are of getting recruitment wrong, both for the individual and for the employer – especially in small companies.

As I have referred to already, it is important when recruiting to maintain a cultural fit. This then raises the question of how suitable candidates are who want to transition out of large corporate environments. My inclination is against recruiting people with backgrounds exclusively in large businesses. Much of what happens in that environment is far removed from the reality of smaller concerns. Of course, some executives can make the transition. And some exposure to big business can be very useful in one way, as it gives experience of good governance, very developed reporting standards and sophisticated methodologies. Many, however, become all too used to reassuring bureaucracy, corridors of comfy offices, vast internal support systems (HR, IT, PAs and so on). In big companies there are always plenty of people to 'do' things, and layers of management to protect individuals from the challenge of having to make and implement decisions quickly. So people working within them often find the cold blast of entrepreneurial organizations too chilly for their taste.

In addition, cost-consciousness is crucial to the success of digital businesses. So it is important to find people who appreciate that priority. That too makes it difficult (but of course not impossible) for people whose sole experience has been in very large companies to fit in. It is a bit like the joke about British government ministers who are allocated cars and drivers as soon as they assume office. So used do they become to this perk that, even after losing office, they will still get into the rear seats of their own 'civilian' cars.

When eBay was recruiting its CEO in 1997, the job Meg Whitman filled, one of the candidates apparently racked up $8,000 of expenses by staying at one of San Francisco's grandest hotels, insisting on first-class travel from the East Coast where he was based, and using a stretched limo to take himself to the eBay office. eBay's founder Pierre Omidyar declared him to be '*the least eBaysian person he had ever met*'.[2]

In very large companies, there are all sorts of remuneration 'extras' that young internet companies cannot usually afford: pension contributions, private health insurance and company cars, for instance. So people used to that are unlikely to find the entrepreneurial approach, which tends to be skewed heavily towards equity, to be attractive. Equity is one of the few advantages that a young company has to offer. By offering shares or share options (equity), there is at least a chance that employees will make a capital sum which can be subject to favourable tax treatment.

It is also hard to recruit from the 'old economy' and big companies for another reason. In many such concerns even a 5 or 10% annual growth rate is considered cracking progress. But this is anaemic for a small business, and unacceptable in the digital economy. While I was CEO of Cheapflights, a 50% annual growth rate was the norm, and that required a state of mind that is difficult to find in older, more established businesses.

One recruitment tool that is worth consideration, certainly at the senior management level, is psychometric testing. If used properly, this can provide very useful insights into a candidate's personality and can be very helpful in ensuring that he or she is right for you and will succeed within the business.

But care is needed. All too often such tests are used flippantly or by people with no real understanding of them. It is vital when using psychometrics to employ a person who is properly qualified to handle them, has plenty of experience of both administering and giving feedback and, most importantly, adheres to a recognized code of ethics.

In recruiting, I have used a number of tests including the Hogan Development Survey (HDS) and the Hogan Personality Inventory (HPI). These help both individuals to gain awareness of how they might appear to others, and managers to understand how best to manage those individuals. Some key leadership qualities, often seen as strengths, can, when overdeveloped, be seen as a 'dark side'.

Such characteristics as enthusiasm, shrewdness or carefulness can be 'bright' or 'dark' (volatility, mistrustfulness, caution). It is important that senior executives recognize their own 'dark side' behaviours, often revealed at a time of stress, as they can be very damaging and undermine a business. Self-awareness helps balance properly these two sides, which if well managed can be a source of strength.

As the internet is, by its very nature, a highly-pressurized environment, inflicting daily stresses and strains, such analysis, awareness and coaching become even more important.

Tests can also be used by external coaches to help team building. As unbiased parties, coaches can also help to resolve the sort of minor conflicts that always exist within companies.[3]

Motivating and retaining the team

The types of people who work well in the internet are those who share a passion for the product and delighting the user, who have a spirit of creativity accompanied by strong commercial drive as well, of course, as possessing the will to win and the self-confidence not to be cowed by sometimes far better-financed competitors.

As small companies grow, so the issue of staff retention becomes more and more important. Whatever the economic conditions, your best people will always get approached, and paying more money is not always sufficient to retain them. So keeping talent is something that every entrepreneur needs to consider very carefully. Of course, stock options have been historically important.

Very early on at Cheapflights we implemented a share option scheme for everyone in the company. That was at a time when we simply could not offer market salaries; so options were not a luxury but an essential part of the compensation package.

In companies with outside investors, the implementation of employee share options schemes (which of course are dilutive to their ordinary or preferred shares) are often seen as a low priority. Outside investors like to talk about share options – but somehow it is one of the board topics that they like to leave 'until the next time'. So, recognizing their motivational power as well as their role in basic compensation for small businesses, it is up to the CEO to argue for them and then to make sure that they are granted.

Increasingly, companies need not only to consider financial rewards for their teams but also how to make the working environment in its broadest sense as attractive as possible.

In this context a good idea I borrowed from my time at Bain & Co. was the concept of the 'mentor'. The principle was simply that each new Cheapflights recruit would be allocated a senior and experienced 'Cheapflighter', not in his or her management chain, with whom the new person could have frank and open conversations and air any issues. I allocated a little budget so that mentors could take their 'mentees' out to lunch from time to time to create a cordial atmosphere in which a proper discussion could take place. The aim here was to give new recruits every opportunity to succeed, and, if they were facing problems, to use the wisdom of more experienced colleagues to help guide them, rather than leave them dangling and demotivated.

Promoting from within is also a powerful motivator and Cheapflights has always tried to do this. One of our earliest recruits is a great example of successful internal promotion. In October 2000, we saw the need to get someone in to help us with web development. We hired a young person, 19 years old, who was working for Greenwich Council on a government start-up initiative to service small businesses with translation and interpretation services. He was 'Employee Number Seven'.

It became clear very early on that this was no ordinary guy. He had in fact been playing around with computers since the age of seven. He really got into them because he used to play a game called *Prince of Persia*. By the age of nine, he was programming his own simple games.

His original job title was 'web developer' and he became a classic example of someone with strong entrepreneurial instincts who was quickly promoted. He started off being responsible for the small 'accommodation' section on the Cheapflights website. Being young and extremely keen, he helped the small business in any way he could and quickly became the onsite technical support for the six-strong team at Cheapflights, dealing with just about any problem – from a toolbar going missing to massive network failures. We then formalized this IT role which meant we were no longer dependent on the outside consultancy that had hitherto provided support.

As the company's user traffic shot up, our young colleague started to hire his own front-end web development team.

He understood very early on the extraordinary power of search marketing as a driver of website traffic. So he started to pay a lot of attention to this new skill set which the internet demanded. This was very helpful for me because I was the person originally responsible at Cheapflights for handling online marketing and the company's (then rather primitive) efforts on GoTo (later Overture), eSpotting (the then new British pay-per-click platform) and, of course, Google.

By 2002 I handed over the keys to our Google AdWords and other online marketing platforms, and promoted him to online marketing manager. At this time he was the only dedicated marketing resource within the company. His deep understanding both of search engine optimization and of pay-per-click campaigns and Cheapflights' increasing global presence meant another promotion in due course to global head of online marketing.

When a company is small, communication is easy. Everyone knows what his or her colleagues are up to. But as the company grows you need to make an effort to talk to everyone regularly – especially the more junior people who do not report directly to the CEO. I have found that they often know more about what is happening than their managers. There is no substitute for team gatherings when the good and the bad news are openly discussed. Everyone in an internet company should be aware of how the company is performing, both on a financial basis and by looking at detailed user metrics. I recently came across an internet company that was losing money at a furious rate. What was shocking was not so much the fact of losses (it is, alas, quite common in digital companies) but that the CEO had not shared the reality of his 'cash burn' with any of his small team.

The internet business really does rely on creativity and every employee should be encouraged to think about the business and submit ideas. Like many other companies, Cheapflights offered prizes for good suggestions. We gave out vouchers redeemable at the luxury hotel group 'Relais et Châteaux' for exceptional performance. On one occasion, we had a company-wide poll on which colleague had been 'most helpful' all round. The winner received round-trip holiday flights for himself and his partner to the Indian Ocean island of Reunion.

Find every way you can to break down barriers between colleagues and overcome the common functional 'silo' effect where, for example, programmers might never talk to sales people and web designers might never meet the finance team.

As the Cheapflights team comes in all sorts of sizes and shapes, as well as levels of fitness, when it came to bonding, I wanted something in which everyone could participate. So the Cheapflights 'Sports Day' was born. This involved all manner of contests from arm-wrestling, to surfing a rubberized wave machine, through to the traditional three-legged race and 'rounders', a game (a little like baseball) played in England since Tudor times.

Birthday lunching was another early idea. Every month I would take out to lunch colleagues whose birthdays fell within that month. This ensured a complete cross-section of attendees. It was truly random.

And on his or her birthday itself, everyone (including me) had the very special honour of wearing the Cheapflights Birthday Hat, a wonderful velvet, multi-coloured affair shaped like a birthday cake complete with battery-powered candles.

Also every month, Cheapflights hosted drinks at the pub – an opportunity for everyone to socialize. Sometimes we added a 'pub quiz' to add to the merriment.

The traditional Christmas office party offers other opportunities. It is always worth considering how best to promote rewards which link to performance. For example, one successful British entrepreneur uses monthly performance sales targets. Every time the sales team hits these monthly targets, the company buys one more case of beer for the Christmas party. They have a visible (and growing) stack of beers in the office. It worked so well that visiting clients, stumbling over the cases, started to remark upon the profusion of the beverage.

Location, location, location

Silicon Valley has to date been the central focus of internet activity. This is hardly surprising given its history as a home for technology companies from Hewlett Packard to Intel to Cisco. Many of the world's leading internet companies have thrived in Silicon Valley, Google and Yahoo being prominent examples.

Silicon Valley provides a happy mix of technology talent, venture funding, a benign climate and, of course, the blessing of light touch

American labour law which means it is easier to hire and fire than in most other parts of the world. Silicon Valley is dynamic, entrepreneurial, innovative and financially successful. It has become a model that the rest of the world is keen to follow.

So this begs the question: is it essential to be in Silicon Valley? I believe the answer is most definitely not. Some years ago, I listened to the founder of Red Hat Inc., an S&P 500 software company, explain why locating his corporate HQ in Raleigh, North Carolina, was an advantage. He cited proximity to talent as well as *not* being in the Silicon Valley maelstrom which encouraged employees to move from company to company far too often! The (American) founder of a successful internet-related company based in Cardiff recently made very similar points.[4]

The UK is actually a good place to hire talent, with both technology and media strongly represented. London, with its vibrant nightlife, in particular remains a magnet. It has the benefit of not only the English language, the lingua franca of the internet, but also a wide range of other skills which makes it a good place from which to launch European expansion. London is now home, for example, to 150,000 French people and, in 2007, was ranked as the 'seventh largest French city'.[5]

As Hugo Burge put it, '*London is a humming technopolis luring young entrepreneurs from across the European Union.*'[6] In contrast, while close to the vast Asia-Pacific region, Silicon Valley is distant from Europe's multi-lingual and highly-developed internet market of 300 million people.

London is also becoming a centre for venture funding (a subject in which I will be providing more detail later), with several of the American firms setting up shop in the city, most notably Accel. Benchmark (which invested in Betfair, Habbo and Bebo among others) has a London office which became sufficiently strong that in 2007 it spun off and is now called Balderton after the tiny London street in which its office is located.[7]

And in good economic times, of course, London gives internet companies the chance to float on the main London Stock Exchange or one of its two junior markets, AIM and the PLUS market.

But there are, of course, other centres of internet excellence outside Silicon Valley, most notably Massachusetts, with its huge concentration of universities including Harvard and MIT, and again its accessibility to finance. Tripadvisor, the American hotel reviews site (sold to Expedia in 2004) is located in Cambridge, Massachusetts. Monster.com, the jobs website is based in Maynard, Massachusetts. And if you have any doubt at all about the chances of internet success outside Silicon Valley, just consider Amazon, located in rainy Seattle in the state of Washington not too far from that other technology giant that avoided the allure of Northern California, Microsoft, on whose office campus travel internet company Expedia was conceived.

Of course, provided that there is the basic infrastructure in place, you can locate an internet business just about anywhere. But I favour places where you can find talent within a relatively easy commute (and that probably means being near eminent universities or at least somewhere where the most highly skilled wish to live), somewhere that is vibrant and fun for the team to work in (do not underestimate the allure of partying for what is likely to be a predominantly young team), and lastly being not too far from a 'money hub'.

In the critical task of building team spirit and staff morale, office space is critical. The Googleplex in Mountainview, California, is perhaps an ideal. It is not grand at all but displays a sort of 'shabby chic' which is functional, professional and 'cool' all at the same time. There is also a swimming pool which may seem an extravagance. But think about all of this from Google's perspective: you want fit and healthy people and you want them to put in long working hours. Feeling well looked after will promote this.

Most internet companies do not (sadly) enjoy Google's profits and cash flows. But there are small cost-effective ways to look after your team and make sure that they feel appreciated. Decent chairs are an example. Working at computers is bad for the back so good supportive chairs are a must. Quite early on, I ditched the cheap chairs and replaced them with ergonomic Aerons® (which had been much mocked during the internet boom as a mark of excess). In terms of productivity, I believe there has been a big return on that investment. We even went one step further and provided a regular and very popular massage service.

Internet offices do not need to be palatial. But I do believe it is important for internet companies to consider very carefully where they locate and what type of office they occupy. There is always a balance between a pleasant working environment and costly frills.

Fountains and atriums are a no-no. Cheapflights started out in Wandsworth, South London, simply to be near the founder's house and to ensure a smooth transition as he handed over the reins after he sold the business in early 2000. It was a perfectly pleasant area but the office was a serviced one (so expensive on a square foot basis), the rooms were small and dark and, with poor public transport connections, it was problematic to reach for many of the employees. So I resolved to move more centrally as soon as we could afford to do so.

Our first move in February 2001 was to Notting Hill, a wonderfully trendy area made famous in the Hugh Grant movie of the same name. We actually occupied the London office of Boxman.com, a competitor to Amazon that had gone spectacularly bankrupt. The Boxman office was extremely pleasant and had a large balcony. When the summer came round we used it for barbecues complete with music. I never did find out what the neighbours thought.

By 2003 Cheapflights was growing so fast that we needed to move once again. We looked at many different areas in central London and finally settled on Marylebone. Located on a former hunting ground of the Tudor King Henry VIII, it is one of the pleasantest parts of central London, sitting between two royal parks, Regent's Park and Hyde Park. It has pastry and coffee shops galore. People like working there.

I have been to many internet offices that just get it plumb wrong. Take the case of one American company, now one of the most successful and best-managed internet travel companies in the world. In its early years, it stumbled. During that period, it opened an office in London with perhaps 50 or more people. I visited the premises on a sales call. I simply could not believe the opulence of the Mayfair building it occupied (Mayfair has some of the most expensive office space in the world) or the contrast which it offered to the little south London room where Cheapflights at that time was located. The reception area was several times bigger than the whole Cheapflights office. My smartly dressed host was a delightful American who had recently arrived in London. I asked him about the Mayfair location. He responded that it was a short walk from his Belgravia home. Obvious!

A few months after I had visited it and marvelled, the parent company closed it down completely.

Outsourcing

One by-product of the fierce British employment legislation has been the availability of outsourced talent. If you cannot shed people easily and quickly, it reduces your business risk to 'outsource' key tasks. In the early days of Cheapflights, it seemed sensible to use outsourcing. Hatt was able to build up the company in his tiny attic only because he could outsource many of the core functions. While he did the selling, design and PR himself, with the help of an excellent and experienced PA (self-employed of course), technology, web development and the Cheapflights discussion board were all outsourced. He used one company to manage the website and another to handle the company's flights database. Hatt used Doubleclick to sell banner ads. With this virtual organization, Cheapflights became a top-10 UK travel website. The total capital investment was one computer. It was a classic 'bootstrapped operation', a 'virtual organization' which allowed Hatt to keep overhead and set-up costs to a bare minimum.

After I took over, I continued the outsourcing policy for technology. All three of my first full-time recruits were for the sales team. This enabled me to crank up the revenues but it did have a disadvantage in these early years. The corporate DNA was very much centred on the sales/commercial operation and technology did lag.

There is no right answer to whether or not to outsource. It is perhaps a safer option in an early-stage business and can be a cheaper alternative especially with the high cost of employment in the UK. Every time the UK government increases the National Insurance tax on income, this strengthens the case. A halfway house is 'offshoring' technology. The team can still be employed in the business: they simply work at a distance. I am involved with small internet companies on both sides of the Atlantic today where the technology is developed either by full-time employees or by contractors in Israel, Poland, Serbia and Russia.

Ultimately it makes sense for most key functions to be full-time locally-recruited individuals. One advantage of being in London is that it does attract a huge pool of talent from all over the world. That is the path we have taken at Cheapflights as we made the transition from Hatt's contracted-out virtual operation to an international business where all the technology is done in-house.

Professional advisers and company boards

The right professional advisers are crucial for those building up internet companies and their selection is an important people issue.

Here my advice is simple. Be sure that you are getting the very best for any particular task and that you are not paying over the odds. It is always worth negotiating on professional fees, and one of the virtues of a difficult economic climate is that outside professionals are more likely to be willing to be flexible on their charges.

Every business needs a good outside accountancy firm, and of course these come in all varieties. Perhaps the key here is to find one that is suitable for the size of business. There is no point hiring Deloittes or PwC if the business is tiny. There are many excellent small accounting companies around. So, shortlist a few, meet the partners and take up references. If they have had experience of fast-growing internet businesses, so much the better.

The same is true for lawyers. There are probably two essential areas for any UK internet business to cover very early on: employment (this includes contracts, hiring, firing and share options) and the highly-specialized but crucial area of intellectual property. Again, it pays to shop around, meet the partners and take up references.

The other 'people' element that is crucial to the success of internet companies, with their constant need to adapt, is the board of directors.

In internet companies I have come across unwieldy boards often because those who invest often demand board seats as non-executive directors (NEDs). The danger is that sometimes such investors are clueless about how the digital economy works. I know of one board where a director, a wealthy and successful businessman in his own 'old economy' field, simply could not grasp the importance of acquiring domain names. His view was that it was a waste of money. This led to some robust conversations. The internet-savvy view ultimately prevailed but it not only used up valuable time, it also cost that company several important domain names which were snapped up by others during the seemingly interminable discussions.

Another example was a non-executive who was a qualified accountant and had spent time as an auditor. He barraged the hard-working finance director on a daily basis with what he thought were helpful tips on prudent financial management. Actually, all this achieved was to bog down the finance director in a sea of emails, each demanding complex financial data to no particular purpose, creating a significant distraction to his day job. There was a huge sigh of relief all round in the company when the non-executive stepped down.

Board meetings should not be time-consuming, acrimonious and sad affairs which serve only to waste time and energy. It is important to have a small, balanced, cohesive board which provides oxygen to the management team rather than trying to smother it with a pillow of demands. I now sit on a number of digital media company boards, including some that are venture-backed. Short board meetings with an emphasis on major strategic or governance issues always work best.

It is useful to get senior team members in front of the board just as it is good to get the board interested in the everyday operations of the company. But the board of directors must not get involved in minutiae and it is best to hold these operational sessions separately from the board meetings themselves.

I increasingly ask myself how non-executive directors (NEDs) can best contribute. Several golden rules spring to mind.[8]

First, the role of NEDs is primarily to protect shareholders' interests; help set strategy; and monitor executive performance in achieving that strategy. But particularly in small companies, they need to contribute something else too. This could be industry expertise, useful connections or prior experience of growing early-stage businesses. I have a co-NED, on one board on which I sit, who is a very experienced and highly rated finance director. His knowledge of complex financial management on a global scale is a hugely valuable and highly welcome resource.

Second, NEDs must not micromanage. There is nothing more irritating for executives than day-to-day interference with the detailed running of their companies.

Many executives who have only worked in large companies and organizations fall at this first hurdle. For example, I recall on one board on which I sat we had an NED from a large, blue-chip management consultancy. Although very accomplished in his own field, he simply could not adjust. He demanded rafts of detailed analysis before any decisions could be made. For a small, dynamic business, this is worse than impractical. It is suffocating.

Third, NEDs should not be clones or cronies of the CEO. They should be genuinely independent and offer complementary skills. For small companies as much as for large ones executive directors should be properly challenged and engaged in making objective decisions.

In sum, take the interviewing process for the board very, very seriously. Getting rid of the wrong NEDs can be a painful and time-consuming affair – so it really is worth getting the appointment right. Good NEDs can provide valuable support.

The sorcerer's apprentice

In 1797 Goethe wrote a poem called *Der Zauberlehrling*, better known by its English translation *The Sorcerer's Apprentice*. In the poem, a sorcerer leaves his young apprentice with chores to carry out, including fetching water in bucketfuls from a well to fill a bath. The apprentice, full of enthusiasm, has the bright idea of using magic to get this tedious task done. Because he has spent some time with the sorcerer, the apprentice feels confident about his own expertise in the magical arts, and is eager to have a go. He decides to cast a spell on a broom to carry out the task of filling the bath on his behalf, which he proceeds to do.

All starts well. But soon the floor is awash as the broom resolutely continues to fetch bucket after bucket of water when the bath is already full. The situation begins to spiral out of control. Eventually the house is completely flooded and the apprentice realizes he must do something. *It dawns on him that he did not cast the spell quite correctly. Worse, he does not know a spell to put things right.*

Not knowing what to do about the now out-of-control broom, the apprentice decides to try stopping it by chopping it up with an axe, cutting it in two. This turns out to be a bad move. Each of the pieces becomes a new broom, both now fetching water, which simply accelerates the flooding. When all seems lost, with a torrent of water flowing through the house, the sorcerer returns. He quickly breaks the spell, gets the situation under control and saves the day. The poem finishes with the sorcerer ordering the broom back into the cupboard and telling it that it will only work again if he calls on it to do so.

This poem is something of a warning to all entrepreneurs, but particularly those in digital media. As with the apprentice, the entrepreneur's idea may be a great one. It takes initiative and nerve to get started: raising some seed funding perhaps, locating an office, identifying a suitable domain name, and so on. And all may go well to begin with. But enterprises develop and take on a life of their own. Like the unstoppable broom, things like, for example, further funding needs, unexpected competition, getting invoices paid, technology advances, and hosting problems can start to swirl around the business. Often inexperienced entrepreneurs grope inexpertly for solutions to these problems, sometimes only making things worse, or at best delaying remedial action as the situation deteriorates. Like the sorcerer, a seasoned manager has experience of problem solving – the less glamorous perhaps, but critical soft underbelly of a business.

Internet businesses, like all businesses, need managing. This is especially true in digital business as the speed of change and the low barriers to entry mean that excellent management is even more crucial for durable success. That is why skills and experience do matter so much. Enthusiasm, energy and initiative, while important ingredients, are in themselves inadequate, as the sorcerer's apprentice soon discovered. He actually just made things worse and worse. He needed the steady and calm hand of experience to sort out the mess.

So what can an entrepreneur draw from this chapter to help him build a profitable company?

- Leadership is vital
- Recruiting is a process that requires time and effort
- Motivation is key to retaining the best talent: and that is not just about money
- Location is important but you do not need to be in Silicon Valley
- Care about your office space
- Consider outsourcing, especially in the early stages

- Ensure you get the right advisers
- Do not underestimate the significance of your board – a good board can spur on a business, a poor one can suffocate it
- Make sure that you have all the necessary experience in your team.

Chapter Five

THE CASH

Annual income twenty pounds, annual expenditure nineteen pounds nineteen and six, result happiness. Annual income twenty pounds, annual expenditure twenty pounds nought and six, result misery.

Mr Wilkins Micawber (Charles Dickens'
***David Copperfield,* 1850)**

One issue which most entrepreneurs face is how to raise money. This chapter looks at how best to do this. Too many companies in the early years of the internet failed because they were unsuccessful at managing their cash. I show how to plan properly, how to manage your cash effectively and how to keep your costs under control. Finally I will look at how you can make money from your efforts by means of an exit.

Raising money

Some businesses never require any external funding. These are ones that are funded by their founders either with cash or 'sweat equity' (the founder does all the work but the quid pro quo is he gets to keep the equity). Some internet businesses only need a little funding, especially if the technology is cheap to build or if it can monetize quite quickly.

Cheapflights is quite unusual in that it has never raised any money (apart from its never-spent £1m buffer fund – see below) and has relied on its own generated cash to finance its expansion. The big advantage of this is that it has avoided diluting the shareholders. The disadvantage is of course that the business, especially in the early years, was very cash constrained. We tried early on to diversify into hotel and holiday price comparison and created websites for this purpose. But we simply could not afford to support the investment in these businesses as well as successfully expand in the huge American market with our core flights comparison service. So we sold off these websites (happily at a profit) but missed out on an opportunity which was seized upon by others. For instance, both TripAdvisor, founded in 2000 (and later acquired by Expedia), and its European rival Trivago, founded in 2004, are profitable, growing businesses providing hotel price comparison.

You do not necessarily need a lot of cash to get started. The costs now of launching an internet site are minimal. I am constantly hearing stories about small internet companies which have started up for a song, have found a good way to monetize and are doing great business. One well-known example is MoneySavingExpert .com, founded in 2003 by financial journalist Martin Lewis. He claims that his initial outlay was £100. His revenue model is paid-for links to finance comparison websites. Lewis's website is visited by eight million people every month. His monthly email, *Martin's Money Tips*, has 3.8 million subscribers. And he has not spent a penny on advertising.[1]

The ideal approach is to do, for instance, what Cheapflights' Hatt and TrustedReviews' Chappell did, which was to manage their businesses with a very low cost base and largely on their 'sweat equity'. To do this, and not run short of funds, means you have to build up a strong cash flow and, at the same time, develop an almost fanatical focus on cost control.

The success of this model has been demonstrated by companies such as TrustedReviews (sold to Time Warner), MoneySupermarket (which went public in 2007), and Craigslist, the giant online classified ads website.

My own view is that, for another reason, it is often better for entrepreneurs to grow without raising funds. It is easier to build a business with a small group of shareholders. There will be fewer opinions to reconcile, lighter administration and less time required for managing investor relationships. Also it avoids dilution of precious equity. You also need to be careful about shareholders outside the founder and management group. Large external shareholders will frequently have different views on strategy and timing from those of founder entrepreneurs. They can also put pressure on companies to spend the money raised quickly, and that is not always a good thing. Bootstrapped businesses generally allocate funds more effectively than venture capital-backed businesses. The search for profit on limited resources drives more efficient financial planning and operations.

And lastly, venture capitalists are very expensive. They will negotiate hard on the terms (and they are very expert at that) and often they will even charge 'management fees' to companies which need every penny to expand their businesses. They will certainly want board representation and certain control and veto rights. They will seek anti-dilution clauses. That is to say, if a subsequent investment round is done at a price lower than the previous investment round then they will receive more shares.

They will try to lock in entrepreneurs for a minimum period of time. There might also be penalties should the entrepreneur leave the business early. Obviously, they want to ensure that the entrepreneurs stay with the business in which they are investing. Typically, venture capitalists do not like founders taking cash out of the company until an exit. They want founders to be focused on their business, not out buying fast cars or in their parlance, 'going to the beach'! In a word, the days of an entrepreneur's blissful independence will come to a juddering halt.

If you really do need to raise money, before you even think about venture capitalists, explore other early-stage sources of finance. The classic sources are 'friends and family' and angel investors. In the UK now, angel investors include many who themselves have had successful digital media backgrounds and can provide useful expertise and contacts to nascent companies. Typically they will invest up to £250,000.

The advantage of avoiding venture capital is that you will retain a large measure of management independence, including the ability to run a 'lifestyle business', if that is what you want, with minimal interference. And of course you do not have to engage in the time-consuming, often frustrating and occasionally even humiliating process of pitching to venture capitalists. The documentary film *Start.up.com* – to which I alluded earlier in this book – has some delightful and instructive 'fly on the wall' scenes as the entrepreneurs pitch to raise finance for their fledgling enterprise from some of the best-known names in Silicon Valley and in Boston. One of the more memorable comments was when one brutal VC told the young founders that he thought that the name of their website 'GovWorks.com' (of which they were very proud) sucked.

So why do companies go out to raise capital? Mainly the reason is to achieve scale as quickly as possible and before a less well-financed competitor has the opportunity to put you out of business. Remember that there are only two sorts of internet company: the quick and the dead. Money is helpful to achieve technology leadership, to attract a high-grade team and to help market the business. Money enables you to develop a cross-border business very quickly. And, of course, all this means is that you are more likely either to achieve a large 'trade' exit (selling out to a company) or a public one (via an initial public offering or IPO).

But while the money might be the principal reason to talk to venture capitalists there are many other ways in which they can be of assistance to growing firms. Certainly, there is a PR element (the 'halo effect' if they have had any big past successes); their extensive networks can be useful when it comes to hiring talent or developing business partnerships; and, when it comes to the exit, this is a process in which they will have a great deal of experience. Additionally, they instill proper reporting disciplines as well as help structure organizations appropriately.

Venture capitalists come in all sorts of shapes and sizes and it is sensible to do as much due diligence on them as they will undoubtedly do on you. There is even now an online review site called 'the Funded.com' which rates the venture capitalists and contains some fairly forceful opinions, both in favour and against, depending on the reviewing entrepreneur's experience. So do speak to other entrepreneurs who have raised venture capital money. Look at who the venture capital partners are and whether they bring relevant experience, and look at what else they have invested in. Some venture capitalists specialize in early-stage finance and some prefer more mature businesses. Make sure you approach the right type to avoid wasting time.

Venture capitalists, like most professional groups, do like their jargon. They toss around terms such as 'B' rounds, 'convertible loans' and 'seed capital' which can be bewildering to entrepreneurs. There are various stages of funding that a company can seek. The earliest stage is 'seed capital' which typically will not involve venture capitalists who will come in later perhaps at the £1m level with an 'A' round. Further rounds of capital-raising may be designated 'B', 'C', 'D' and so on and can involve tens of millions of pounds.

At the time of writing, the British online grocery retailer Ocado has had no fewer than seven fund-raising rounds with a total investment thus far of £350m. One recent round was for £50m with investors including Fidelity and Generation Investment Management (ex-Vice President Al Gore's fund), which invested £7m.[2]

Competing with giant established grocery chains such as Tesco in online delivery is certainly an expensive business, as you have to build up an entire infrastructure from scratch. This is hardly an ambition that can be satisfied from friends and family, or indeed angel investors!

Likewise, Facebook is certainly one of the success stories of the internet's second decade. But this success has not come on the cheap. Facebook has raised prodigious quantities of money, estimated at over $600m over four years, attracting a raft of premier league investors including Accel, Greylock and, more recently, Microsoft.[3]

Venture capitalists do not, as a rule, favour 'Ordinary shares' which give the same rights to all investors (in contrast these will be the sorts of shares which angels and friends and families typically accept).

Venture capitalists will consider:

- 'Preferred shares' which simply means that the venture capitalists get a claim prior to those of the ordinary shareholders on assets in the event of liquidation.
- Bridge funding, often in the form of convertible loans, which can fill the gap between equity raising, often converting into shares at a discount to the next funding round.

Be ready to put a lot of time into fundraising. The process can take months. You need to be prepared, very prepared. It is a good idea to 'get your house in order' pre-deal: for instance, files must be in good shape and accounts up to date. Understand exactly why you need the money and what you are you going to do with it. You need to prepare carefully for 'the pitch' and be sure that you can answer whatever questions come up.

Venture capitalists like businesses that grow very fast and, best of all, those that will grow even faster when their money has been invested. And whatever they say about 'passing' on great investments, they do not like doing so. No one wants to be like the venture capital firm in California that decided to pass on eBay. Rather they want to be like Benchmark which invested $5m for 21.5% of the company, a stake that would eventually be worth $4bn.[4]

So, when pitching, entrepreneurs should not hesitate to sell the dream. If the venture capitalists do not invest *right now*, they *will* miss the *big* one. After all, what is the point of going to them if you yourself do not believe that your company, your idea, will indeed be the next big one?

President Lyndon Johnson once said:

> *You've got to believe in what you are selling. What convinces is conviction. You simply have to believe in the argument you are advancing; if you don't, you're as good as dead. The other person will sense that something isn't there.*

If you lack conviction in front of venture capitalists, you will be toast.

If you do need to raise money, it is easier to raise it when you are not struggling to survive. You will be familiar with how it is easier to get a credit card or overdraft when you have plenty of money in the bank. It is much harder to obtain one when you have very little cash and you most urgently require a debt facility, due to the risk you present to the lender. This problem repeats itself through the echelons of funding.

Do not wait until the well is dry – plan funding early. Do not wait for a crisis.

Planning

One of the great weaknesses of early internet businesses was poor budget planning. This is a necessity at any stage of a business's development. At Cheapflights we always worked to a very detailed one-year budget. At the FTSE 100 company where I worked in the 1980s, the three-year budget and plan was an enormous document that took me three months to produce (with the help of a 12-strong department). At Cheapflights, planning in the early years was quite primitive but, as time has gone on, the process has become more elaborate (and time-consuming).

It is impossible to know if the business is doing well or badly unless you have a budget against which to measure it. And the budget will tell you ahead of time when the periods of spend and cash need are greatest so that you can be fully prepared. They should build in seasonality. So, for example, when Cheapflights was purely a UK business, December was the worst sales month in the year and January the best. Sales could (and did) double in a month. When Cheapflights expanded into the USA, the vibrant pre-Thanksgiving flights market was a welcome offset to the UK's typically subdued autumn period. Seasonality takes some time fully to understand.

This is another reason why it is important to get your reporting in good order and to report monthly.

We knew and understood these monthly differences and were not alarmed by them.

One important overriding rule for budgets is to overestimate costs and underestimate sales. This is important as so many internet companies take their budgeted sales number as some sort of certainty, get really excited about this high level of (future) growth, and then of course spend, spend, spend in anticipation of the surging sales number. Sadly sales are always rather uncertain whereas costs should be more predictable. Not only do entrepreneurs often exaggerate sales growth, they are also simply unaware of where costs may lurk in their business. So do not spend based on 'hockey stick' sales projection curves or you will risk problems. Do not forget that growing companies tend to swallow cash, so plan for working capital issues caused by fast growth. It does not matter how profitable you are, profits are not the same thing as cash and are no substitute for it. It is cash that pays the salaries, rent, tax, suppliers and so on.

It is prudent to build up cash reserves in case of problem months. Make sure you understand your cash conversion cycle. This is simply the duration of time it takes a firm to convert its activities requiring cash back into cash returns. It will help you manage cash better and possibly put off the need for funding. Understanding the company's cash conversion cycle can enable founders to work out whether they can access short-term funding from their customers as they grow (customers pay upfront, expenditure happens later), or whether instead they might face increasing cash constraints with growth (expenditure happens upfront, customers pay later).

And make sure that you 'provision' adequately. When you incur costs, for example for legal advice, you may not receive an invoice straight away. It is very sensible to make a provision for this invoice (account for a provisional cost) based on your best estimate of what this might be (often exact, sometimes not) and when it is likely to be paid. This helps improve the accuracy of your financial planning.

One important provision is for likely bad debts. Cheapflights has had, by necessity, to become a master of credit control. For the travel industry is notoriously fickle. Small companies regularly go under. Big companies can crash unexpectedly. So, based on 14 years of experience, we can now provision quite accurately for bad debts. Again, this helps to prevent nasty surprises at the year end.

When it comes to spending the precious cash, have one person control all spending and be accountable for that expenditure. That same person should open all the post to check for bills and should date stamp all incoming mail. At Cheapflights this was almost a religion. Even my Christmas cards were opened by the zealous finance department and date-stamped.

Set up monthly pay runs and, if paying by cheque, make sure you monitor these payments and keep a record of them. Some suppliers may take a while to pay in cheques. A cheque reconciliation is therefore very important, especially in businesses with modest amounts of cash available, to ensure that you have sufficient funds in hand on the day they do pay it in. Bounced cheques can be damaging to relationships with suppliers.

The relationship with the bank is important. Find an appropriate bank for your needs and develop a good rapport with the manager. This is very important when discussing possible credit needs or credit cards. Also, banks are vicious about fees, and you will need carefully to monitor any unnecessary fees on transactions. Plan with the bank in case of working capital issues that come with growth. And of course check the bank balance every day at least.

Cash is king

Understanding the importance of cash in the business cannot be overstated. It is very surprising how many early-stage businesses, driven by entrepreneurs with a sales or technology background, simply forget about cash.

The first essential is proper reporting: sales, costs, and cash flow must be reported daily or weekly, as well as all the usual internet metrics – or key performance indicators – such as traffic and conversions. For any internet company metric reporting is inextricably linked to financial reporting and forms a key guide to the health of the business. Basic internet metrics include unique users (people who visit you at least once a month: if I visit a website three times from my computer during one month I count as one unique user), visits (total number of visits to the website), page impressions (the number of pages visited). Few people talk these days about the number of 'hits': this was never a meaningful measure as web pages could always be constructed to ensure that there was more than one hit in order to exaggerate the traffic received.

This level of reporting is not, I repeat not, a big company affectation.

Conversions are particularly important as this is how you measure users who actually convert to cash, because they are paying for products, clicking on paying links, paying subscriptions or whatever is the chosen revenue model. In the case of Cheapflights it is all very well to have torrents of users, but unless those users click on the flight deals they are of limited value. And if they click too often that is bad because they will not be truly converting for the travel provider who should be monitoring their sales of flight tickets from the leads produced by Cheapflights. So, as I have often had to explain, there is little point in getting friends and relations to click if they are not intending to buy flights, as that would be a sure way to shed paying clients.

I have found over the years that there is often much more emphasis on these general metrics than on the money side of the business. Perhaps it is more fun to say '*I have 100,000 unique users*' (wow, what a large number, well done!) than '*I have £412.14p in sales*' (what?). Sadly though, the metrics, however strong, do not pay the bills. Do not, however, dismiss traffic out of hand. It is a big plus if a website can get traffic – *if* that traffic is cheaply gained and engages with that website. Usually, if it is 'genuine' traffic, you will be able to monetize eventually. Google is the classic example of a company rapidly monetizing on the back of huge traffic. Amazon, by contrast, took years to break into profit but on the back of surging numbers and real engagement with its customers.

Ideally, use proven systems such as Sage, Quickbooks or SAP to manage financial reporting. However busy you are, make sure it gets done and that you generate full monthly reports. In my experience, the better the financial reporting the healthier the company. And it is not a result of size. I have seen internet companies that employ a dozen or even 50 people – and have been around a while – produce far worse reports than an early-stage bootstrapped one-person start-up.

A good finance person is a prerequisite, and it is essential from day one to put in place proper controls. Recently, I came across an internet company that employs 50 people. It had no finance director and I asked the CEO why not. He told me that the company had an excellent bookkeeper and that there was therefore no need for a finance director. I could not have disagreed more. I felt that the financial reporting was very flabby, from its lack of clarity about sales recognition to sloppy budgeting.

There is always a need for a finance director and this should be an important recruiting priority. Of course, good bookkeepers are worth their weight in gold. They are readily available from websites such as gumtree.com. They are not expensive and can save you a lot of time and effort. By employing a bookkeeper right off the starting blocks, you will avoid distraction and misery later on. But a bookkeeper does not have the full range of skills offered by a properly qualified finance director.

If you cannot afford a full-time finance person, hire a part-time one. Finance is not just about bookkeeping. It has a fundamental role to play across all aspects of the business whether helping in pricing policy, checking operating assumptions and budgets (CEOs are usually overoptimistic by nature and need reining in) or negotiating contracts. But perhaps there is one function above all in which a good finance director will prove his worth: minding the cash.

Cheque-signing authority is one area for caution. This varies for every size of business, but the rule of thumb is that larger cheques should always have two signatures so that payments are subject to proper scrutiny. Lord Hanson, a famous British industrialist of the 1980s, always insisted on signing all expenditures over £500 even when his businesses were turning over billions of pounds.

It is a good idea to ensure that capital items are properly thought through and not purchased on the nod. Any capital items should be subject to a proper written paper explaining why the item is to be bought, what efforts have been made to ensure that it offers the best value for money, and what return for the business is expected from the investment. Creating websites is one item for which businesses traditionally have paid far too much. When Ryanair first considered building a website, it received quotations from suppliers for up to £3.5m. Chief executive Michael O'Leary came across two students, one still at school, the other studying to be a dentist. The two students agreed to build the website for £15,500. Having delivered it on time, they were then beaten down by O'Leary to £12,000.[5]

O'Leary is famous for putting attention to cost at the centre of his strategy – although forbidding his staff to recharge their mobile phones while in the office is perhaps a little harsh even by his standards.[6]

Being frugal can often be advantageous to an internet company. Certainly Amazon's Bezos thinks so. For when *Business Week* asked Bezos about innovation, he said:

> *I think frugality drives innovation, just like other constraints do. One of the only ways to get out of a tight box is to invent your way out. When we were [first] trying to acquire customers, we didn't have money to spend on ad budgets. So we created the associates program, [which lets] any website link to us, and we give them a revenue share. We invented one-click shopping so we could make check-out faster. Those things didn't require big budgets. They required thoughtfulness and focus on the customer.*[7]

Too many small businesses (and large ones too) just waste money on unnecessary items. I worked with one small internet business that was using an expensive laser printer (with costly colour cartridges) to perform every-day office print runs. I quickly had it locked away. Cheapflights was famously cautious about stationery costs, another common drain of precious resources. How often have you heard someone say '*I am doing the stationery order: is there anything you want?*' (a gold Cross pen or a perhaps a Mont Blanc propelling pencil?!)

Think about every item of cost. I have an entrepreneur friend who discovered that it was quite unnecessary to buy bottles of water for the water cooler. He had discovered that ordinary London tap water was a perfectly good substitute as it was not the perceived purity of the water that his team wanted but simply water that was chilled. I have never looked at a water cooler again without recalling that gem.

But sometimes cost control can be taken too far. I remember that at the FTSE 100 company I worked for in the pre-internet days, the managing director queried why each member of the business development department needed a copy of the *Financial Times* in the morning. He suggested that we all share one copy until I explained that being up-to-speed on financial news first thing in the working day was a prerequisite of the job. Nevertheless, it was the right question to ask.

So expense control is very important. My own belief is that you need to engender a sense of responsibility in the team and that no amount of form-filling is a substitute for that. In the early days of Cheapflights, one of the sales team, a first-class salesman, entertained a client and managed to amass a bar bill of £1,600. When he confessed this to me on the following day, I am sure that he quite expected to be hauled over the coals. It was probably excessive but at least the recipient of the company's largesse was a long-standing and important client whose business was an important contributor to the bottom line. (But, perhaps to the client's disappointment, the largesse was not repeated.)

Company credit cards are very dangerous items and should be discouraged. I am quite certain that they encourage freer spending than would otherwise be the case.

Almost every company needs the ability to pay by credit card, but do ensure that its usage is controlled carefully by the CEO or FD.

Cash collection

One of the biggest minefields is cash collection. Again, clear reporting is key. Have a very clear idea of how quickly the cash is coming in. Who is slow? And when should the alarm bells be ringing? Think of cash collection as the most important bit of financial reporting you can do: more important than sales, sales pipelines, number of users, page impressions and all the other vital pieces of operating data. Understand fully who is paying too slowly and why, and be sure to keep the pressure up on the slow payers. Do not be shy about sending someone round to pick up overdue cheques in person – and don't be afraid of hiring a debt collection company as a last resort. Better still, avoid cheques – insist instead on online transfers.

Always make sure that your payment terms and conditions are absolutely watertight; otherwise, collections can become tricky. And, of course, always specify payment days on invoices; otherwise you will, more often than not, need to chase for payment. Track 'debtor days' as a key performance indicator (KPI). This simple metric enables you to measure how quickly you collect your cash from suppliers. The formula is:

$$\left[\text{debtors at month end}/\text{sales (last 12 months)}\right]\times 365$$

For example, if your average payment terms are net 30 days (30 days from the invoice date) but your debtor days are 60 days, you are, on average, allowing your customers an extra 30 days to pay their invoices. You may wish to do something about that.

Check the creditworthiness of clients carefully. Be sure to set tight credit limits. If you are not familiar with the client, then do not hesitate to put a small limit to begin with and raise it only gradually as the relationship grows. If you are unable to check the credit of a client – or you have any doubts at all about its creditworthiness – do not be shy about requesting upfront payment. In any case, upfront payment is always best for cash flow.

Do not make the classic error of, having experienced a few months of timely payments, removing the limit and then seeing the debt shooting through the roof, never to be paid. Ongoing client monitoring is very important. Past history of paying is not always an indicator of future solvency. Listen carefully to industry gossip. I once heard about the financial problems of a UK airline some six months before these became public knowledge. I was thus able to manage our financial exposure down to an acceptable level.

Do not allow your sales to be dominated by one client. At Cheapflights we always got a bit nervous if any client accounted for more than 15% of sales in any month, however blue-chip and reliable that client appeared to be. We live in a world where household names like Northern Rock, Royal Bank of Scotland and Woolworths can collapse overnight. And in the travel industry bankruptcy is an all-too-familiar fate. Just remember poor Freddie Laker, the pioneer of low-cost transatlantic air travel, or major American carriers like Eastern, Braniff, PanAm and TWA. In the current world, even governments run out of money. If you cannot rely on Iceland and Dubai World (the government-owned investment arm of the Dubai government) to remain solvent, who can you rely on? It pays to be very cynical about clients.

Try, if possible, to shorten payment terms on sales invoices. Make this part of the negotiation process. It is often worth considering reducing the payment terms in exchange for discounting the price. What you should never do is discount the price and then go easy on payment terms. Above all, never accept the line that *'our payment terms are standard. They are 90 days.'* (Or pick any number!) There is nothing standard about payment terms: if you want to get paid quickly, ask for faster terms and get those terms in writing. Set the rules yourself so that clients play by them and not you by theirs.

Make sure that invoices go out on time. If working with advertising sales networks, ensure that payment terms are from the invoice date, not when they collect cash. Try not to shoulder their debt collection risk. I heard about one digital media business that entered into an arrangement with an advertising sales house in which the terms specified that they (the business) would get the cash within *'30 days of the agency collecting cash from their clients'*. That sounded fine and dandy. But the business overlooked one fundamental point: the collections bit. In practice the relationship was completely unworkable as the business had no visibility at all on the sales house's collections. This became obvious in the first six months of the agreement when less than 5% of the monies owed had been paid.

If you make money from running online ad campaigns, ensure that you have fully delivered the ad campaign (in terms of the number of ad impressions served) in order to avoid having later to issue credit notes to customers.

If taking payment online, it is best to offer more forms of payment rather than fewer, if affordable. Always negotiate on fees per transaction and watch out for setup or annual fees. Payment by mobile telephone is becoming increasingly popular with the rapid take-up of 'smart' phones. But such payment systems can be very expensive to operate. So be sure to understand fully how expensive *before* signing any contracts with mobile phone payment processors.

And do make certain that everyone in the company understands the importance of cash. This is particularly important for a sales force trying to hit its numbers. Do not allow the sales team to promise the earth to its clients in order to meet its targets. Linking sales teams' bonuses to cash collected is a very good way of motivating your sales team to ensure that deals it signs actually do convert to cash at bank quickly. And try to ensure that the sales person who has a warm relationship with a client is not the same person who has to turn up the pressure to get that client to pay. Of course you want clients to pay and to pay quickly, but you do not want to destroy important relationships in that process.

Be sensible about paying bills. Do not get the reputation of being a 'bad payer' as it will come back to haunt you. If you have cash flow problems, it is worth sitting down with your supplier and working out a payment plan. For that reason it is worth building good relationships with your suppliers, especially in their accounts departments. And never be late on your payment to the government. It is quite common to come across short-term PAYE and VAT fiddling in early stage businesses or ones which are struggling. But this is very shortsighted. I came across one internet business where the naive founder thought he could keep the business afloat by delaying PAYE and VAT payments: his outstanding bill to the taxman actually amounted to more than 50% of his annual sales. This was more than a mistake. It was plain idiocy.

The importance of employee options

Professor Milton Friedman famously blamed government profligacy on the fact that it was a case of A (the government) spending B (the taxpayer)'s money on C (whatever the government felt like spending money on). But even in private companies, sometimes staff feel that they are spending other people's money rather than their own. It is much easier for team members to understand the importance of cash and financial prudence if they have options (to buy shares) in the business. Options get rid of the 'us and them' divide ('bosses and workers') or the 'other people's money' profligacy which is prevalent in so much of the public sector. It is important to ensure that your team members understand their options schemes. Options are well known to be extremely confusing. Lots of legalese and paperwork are necessarily involved. The better the understanding that the team has of your scheme, the more aligned its objectives and incentives will be with the business. Most importantly, options incentivise staff without the need to spend cash up front and can substitute for the need to pay high salaries.

Keeping the lid on costs

On the afternoon of 6 November 2000, California-based Pets.com went into liquidation. It had launched in August 1998 and went public in February 2000. Just 268 days later it was bust.

During its first financial year Pets.com spent $11.8m on advertising but its sales amounted to $619,000. In January 2000, Pets.com spent $1.2m on a Super Bowl ad.

But it was not this turbo-charged marketing overspend that was the root cause of its demise. Pets.com's problem was that it was actually selling goods, pet accessories and supplies, for *less* than the price that it paid for them. In other words, as it expanded, so its losses grew and the cash went flying out of the door.

Little wonder then that, in June 2008, CNET ranked Pets.com as one of the greatest dot.com disasters in history.[8]

Much of financial management is about plain commonsense. But internet companies are probably more culpable than most other types of business in lacking commonsense. This is first because the internet is still a relatively new form of business; second, because it is more difficult for hyper-growth companies to maintain financial controls; and last, because of the ludicrous and often chimerical potential valuations that have often clouded management's judgement. It is rather like all those people who used to boast about their house's 'value'. They *felt* wealthy so they went out and spent money forgetting that the value of their house was simply the money someone was prepared to pay for it; and that could change at any given moment.

Internet companies are no different. I can just imagine the conversations at Boxman, the ill-fated European competitor to Amazon whose London office Cheapflights occupied just weeks after its failure. They might have gone something like this:

We are going to float for £300m; so why worry too much about a few million on advertising or tech bills with IBM: small potatoes in the general scheme of things.

Cheapflights' founder Hatt had grown his business with 'sweat equity'. He had never raised any money (not even from friends and family, let alone from venture capitalists) and funded his nascent company out of the money that he was making from it. Not only did he identify a solid revenue stream (selling qualified leads to the travel industry), he also managed the company on a shoestring. No full-time employees. No office. No advertising at all. By early 2000, his website was getting over 300,000 unique users and his hosting costs for the full two years prior to his sale of the business were barely £1,000.

It was this lean approach, which contrasted with so many other dot. coms of the late 1990s, that made Cheapflights such an attractive proposition. If this company could continue to expand – while keeping control over costs and achieving an attractive operating margin – then its potential was enormous.

Hatt had good reasons to sell out. He had worked very long hours over four years. He was not going to expand the business without recruiting a team and I suspect that that was not something which he really wanted to do. And he recognized that internet values were going through the roof. With immaculate timing, we actually purchased the company days before NASDAQ collapsed. We should have waited for a few weeks. But hindsight is a fine thing!

So Hugo Burge, who came from a property and entrepreneurial background, and I arranged a management buy-in. Hugo and I both independently knew close friends of Hatt's so we got to hear about his very private decision to sell. Originally our two consortia were in competition but, in the end, we joined forces, together raising sufficient funds to buy Hatt out for the amount that he required.

The investors in Cheapflights who bought out its founder allocated a million pounds in 'rainy day' money, a buffer for the business in case it hit any weak spots, over and above the money paid to Hatt. To this day, that safety net fund has never been touched and sits in a deposit account with other funds generated by the business. Our working capital was precisely £20,000 – so that was an excellent way to focus the mind on what to spend money on.

One of the first tasks at Cheapflights was to find suitable office space as the business had been operated in Hatt's attic – this rather cramped room was not, of course, included in the purchase price. Many early-stage businesses make the mistake of locking in to long office leases. We decided to begin with a serviced office which was expensive on a square-foot basis but offered a great deal of flexibility. You could add or subtract space with very little notice. Meeting rooms could be hired by the hour. The copying machine was charged on a usage basis.

This first serviced office was very close to Hatt's Wandsworth house. This was extremely helpful in the transition as we learnt all aspects of the business from the founder who dropped in regularly for cups of tea and to give us his critique on how we were doing managing 'his' business.

The message here is that it is impossible to get office space exactly right but it is better to err on the cautious side. Do not occupy large offices on the basis of growth forecasts, however realistic those forecasts may appear. Do work at home to start with. Then stick to serviced offices certainly in the early stages of a business. And, above all, do not sign up for very long leases. Just remember that, say, £10,000 a year for a 10-year lease is a legally binding commitment to the business of £100,000.

Looking for property is time-consuming and highly risky. But it pays to put in the time in order to find the very best deal. Using an agent to help find properties is a good way of saving time and energy. They can often find places that have not formally come onto the market as well as help in the negotiations. Certainly it is worth getting experienced property lawyers to check every word of a lease agreement. They can be full of pitfalls for the unwary.

Even the most experienced business people get caught out by property leases. Rupert Murdoch's NewsCorp was said to be stuck with rental costs of $1m *a month* for offices in Los Angeles to which it planned to relocate MySpace and other digital businesses. Reportedly, the company signed a 12-year lease worth about $350m in August 2008. But then NewsCorp cut the MySpace workforce by 40% and abandoned the office move.[9]

When looking for cheap office space, do not forget to factor in service charges and business rates. It is not uncommon for these to add up to more than the annual rent cost in today's depressed office market.

Hiring people is a major expense. At Cheapflights, we were probably a little late in developing our in-house technology team. In the early years, our resources were very limited. We did employ plenty of outsourced contractors, preferring to put our staff investment into sales and the commercial side of the business. As the business grew and prospered, we were able to correct this and now technology sits on an equal footing within the company.

The pressure to hire is a constant. Senior managers always want more people. Managing large teams often becomes a sign of corporate machismo. It is a CEO's job to prevent any hiring unless it is truly a proven need (very often it is not).

There are many ways to supplement teams. I have always favoured using bright college interns and began that process back in 2000. Cheapflights has had many interns over the years drawn from both schools and universities. Almost always the interns enjoy the experience of working in a dynamic digital media environment. They can be very helpful in supplementing the resources of, for instance, the finance director. And they, almost always, provide good value for money.

Many tasks can be completed by temporary freelancers. At Cheapflights, some of the best of these ended up as full-time staff members. Two of Hatt's outsourced team joined us in due course as employees. Trialling freelancers is an efficient way to mitigate the financial risk of taking someone on full-time while getting the necessary help in a flexible way to meet the specific business needs of the moment.

In Chapter Four, I talked about using headhunters. But of course one great way to save on headhunter fees is to use your own network. LinkedIn is a useful resource too to track down potential recruits.

Other key external relationships are with legal and financial advisers. Both are hugely important but can, like headhunters, be very expensive. Try to do as much internally as possible as it will be cheaper than getting the professional support companies involved. And when you do bring in lawyers and accountants, do understand how they charge and watch carefully for 'mission creep', the broadening of objectives leading to greater and unplanned commitments. Try if possible to get caps put on work they do, otherwise you will soon find yourself in escalating 'pelican' relationships (ones with very large bills attached).

The other big cash drain for young internet companies, apart from people costs, is technology. Don't overspend on technology and in particular hosting. Recently, I came across a small internet company with just a few hundred thousand users that was paying £7,000 a month for hosting. I had an expert take a look at the requirements and it turned out that the job could be done just as effectively for £2,000 a month without affecting the efficiency of the operation one iota.

The key things to consider when choosing hosting are:

- Upfront investment versus monthly cost – important for cash flow
- Security and reliability
- In-house versus outsourced expertise
- Hardware prices. These are dropping fast which is resulting in many more hosting options than ever before. 'Cloud computing' is maturing and rapidly changing the hosting landscape which is especially important for cash-strapped internet start-ups.

For entrepreneurs there are several possible choices (in ascending order of cost):

- Simple hosting: there are of course many basic hosting offerings for blogs and simple websites that cost very little, but these services are not suitable for the majority of online start-ups which will require something more sophisticated.
- Cloud computing: this is led by big names, like Amazon, Google, Microsoft and Rack Space. These platforms offer on-demand resources with a pay-as-you-go cost model, which is very attractive for start-ups. This option does not usually require any upfront payments and prices are calculated based on usage (central processing unit – CPU – cycles, disc space,

bandwidth). These systems provide self-servicing tools for resources and capacity management, but there is often no live support available. This option requires some in-house expertise and learning, but pricing is very attractive.

- Managed hosting: this offers dedicated or shared resources which often include some software licences and also a range of additional services, like backup, raw storage space, database management, security management, 24/7 support. The pricing structure is usually based on monthly fees per service provided and hardware is often offered through leasing deals. In this case, there are no upfront expenses and no need for in-house hardware installation and maintenance expertise, but monthly fees are higher.

- Co-location or self hosting: rent a server rack and dedicated internet connection and buy servers and software licences. It requires some hardware installation and management experience (which adds to the payroll). This option demands higher upfront expenditure, but it is usually more cost effective in the long run for larger and more complex server deployments if you have pre-existing in-house expertise.

If you are not a technology expert shop around and have any quotes reviewed by someone you trust with plenty of suitable experience. This may sound startlingly obvious but you would be surprised how many people do not in fact take the trouble to do this.

The exit

Good. You have successfully 'bootstrapped' (that is, not resorting to any external financial help) a business using just your money. Or you raided the wallets of friends and family or angel investors.

Or you might have raised a few rounds of venture capital funding.

At some stage, your thoughts may turn to '*How do I get some cash for my shares? How do I get some personal liquidity for all my efforts?*' It is never too early to start thinking about an exit but, at the end of the day, you will never be able to dictate the 'right time'. And alas, timing is everything.

There are three classic means to an exit: sale to a financial buyer, sale to a trade buyer, or a stock market flotation (an initial public offering or 'IPO'). Any potential buyer will look for similar characteristics: a strong management team, a robust strategy, a track record of growth, a leading market position, lots of potential for the future and, increasingly, strong monetization. In the early days of the internet, lots of 'eyeballs' (internet jargon for users) and the promise of jam tomorrow was sufficient to underwrite huge valuations. But today, with the exception of some mega-players such as Twitter and Facebook, a strong profit stream is a big advantage.

A word of caution – however attractive your business appears to you (and businesses always seem more attractive to the people who found and then run them than they do to cynical outsiders), there is one way in which an exit can fail completely – one which is totally outside anyone's control – and that is the state of the market. There are times when markets are healthy and strong. Optimism reigns supreme. Lots of money swirls around. Investors enjoy profits and look for reinvestment opportunities. Economies are buoyant. There is strong appetite for risk.

These are clearly the times when it has been relatively easy to exit from a digital business: the period before March 2000 and from 2004 to the summer of 2007 were both windows of opportunity. The NASDAQ crash and more recently the credit crunch and global banking crisis of 2007–2009 both led to tougher exit times. Of course, it is sometimes still possible to exit in a bad market. Even in the rather torrid year of 2009, the online restaurant reservation company OpenTable (which had been founded in 1998) floated successfully on NASDAQ. But exiting in a weak market is much harder, with more limited options available and lower valuations.

A clear example of the importance of timing is French price comparison website Kelkoo. In April 2004, at a time of strong demand for digital properties, Kelkoo was bought by Yahoo Inc. for €450m.

In November 2008, at a time of weak demand, Kelkoo was sold by Yahoo Inc. to the private equity firm Jamplant Ltd for €100m.[10]

Whatever Yahoo may or may not have done to Kelkoo during its four years of ownership, this was a classic example of buying at the peak and selling at the bottom.

Another classic case of *good* timing for the sellers was uSwitch. This was a UK website that pioneered price comparison for household energy bills. It was founded in 2000 by a former PwC financier called Andrew Salmon and Lord Milford Haven, a cousin of the Queen. The site grew very rapidly as household bills soared, and when, in late 2005, there was a major hike in gas prices, it really was a sensible time to sell. So sell they did, to E.W. Scripps the American newspaper group. The price tag was £210m.

Sadly, UK consumers' desire to switch suppliers seems to have tailed off somewhat since those heady days and in August 2009, just four years later, Scripps put uSwitch on the block, apparently with one offer on the table of £15–£20m from none other than Salmon and Milford Haven.[11]

Finally, in December 2009, Scripps announced the sale of uSwitch to Forward Internet Group for 'an undisclosed sum'.[12]

Business owners cannot dictate the condition of the market. They should use the fallow period to focus on operations and consider very carefully what is needed to take advantage of a market upturn.

One useful task is to consider who the exit advisers might be. Here it is important to match the size of the business with the type of adviser. A small business can easily be sold with the advice of a decent lawyer or accountant. A larger business may merit a corporate finance adviser. There are many types from one person boutiques to 'bulge bracket' banks.

If you opt for the trade sale route and want to create some competitive tension, using a corporate finance firm to handle that process is a sensible way of ensuring the best possible deal.

Finding the right corporate finance firm is a matter of seeing what deals they have done and checking them out with both buyers and sellers. Sellers may rave about a particular firm; but if there are buyers out there who are aggrieved because they have paid too much, and those buyers might be the same for your business, do watch out. The ideal is to find a firm that is trusted by both buyers and sellers. The digital world is a small one with few secrets.

The relationship with the deal adviser is a critical factor. Personal chemistry is vital. In any sale, things get very tense so it is worth working with enjoyable and likeable souls. Only by sitting down with them at some length will this become clear.

Take your time to hire the right advisers. Ask around your own contact base, people you know and trust. I recently learned from an internet CEO about an exit process that he had formally started. He went to a meeting with his newly-appointed banker to talk about the sale of his company to a possible purchaser who clearly was not very interested. So the banker commented that if the prospective purchaser didn't like this opportunity, he had another company which might tickle his fancy, and then expounded on it at some length. My source tells me that he fired that firm immediately.

Another incident I heard about was from a company who initiated a trade sale process on a very tight timetable. The senior banker in charge of the deal went away on holiday in the first week of the process without telling his client and leaving those vital early days in the hands of a junior. This was the first sign that the senior banker was not actually going to manage the deal and that he was going to leave it to his much less experienced colleague. Not surprisingly, the whole transaction subsequently faltered.

It is worth having an extensive beauty parade. See how thoroughly they have considered the likely field of potential buyers to determine how wide your options actually are. You will know your business better than they do but it is an interesting reality check on how well they understand your particular sector. It is also an opportunity for them to show their creativity.

You should conduct the same detailed process for lawyers. All companies have lawyers but you should ensure that yours can actually handle exits successfully before simply signing them up because they are there and have the relationship.

Often law firms (unless they are very large) will have strengths in one area but weaknesses in others. Firms that are good, for example in employment law, may not have the commercial track record to handle complex sales.

However good the corporate financiers are, the role of the lawyers is absolutely critical and the sale and purchase agreement tends to end up as a tug-of-war between the two legal teams. You want to be sure that your guy is the one pulling the rope while the others are collapsed on the ground.

One of the big decisions that any successful digital media business has to consider is whether or not to float and that is something about which professional advice is key. The disadvantage of an IPO is that it is extremely expensive and time-consuming. You also need to consider the resulting implications of being a publicly-listed company and all that it entails. But the advantage of considering an IPO is that, at the very least, it broadens exit options and can, if conducted in parallel, make a trade sale that much more focused. There is nothing better to concentrate a trade buyer's mind than knowing that, if he does not bid sufficiently high, you will go to the stock market rather than wait around to accept a reduced price.

The normal lead time for an IPO can be anything from six months up to a year. Internal accounting systems and information have to be brought up to public company standards. If the board is deficient (lacking in 'independent' directors, for example) these people need to be recruited. An investor relations function will need to be built and you will, in all likelihood, need careful and specialized training. Dealing with the public markets is not something best learned by trial and error on the job. The due diligence can easily take a year. The biggest danger to any entrepreneur contemplating an IPO is that the process itself is so time-consuming that it diverts his or her attention from running the business. This is another reason to have a first-rate finance director who should be able to take much of the day-to-day strain.

Working at a listed company is certainly not to every internet entrepreneur's taste. Jason Gissing, one of the founders, and until recently finance director, of Ocado, said '*I would rather shoot myself than be FD of a listed company. I have no interest in it. I can think of no more thankless a task in corporate Britain. I didn't start*

Ocado to sit in a room full of grey suits and have them abuse me about quarterly earnings figures. It's just not what I want to do with my life.[13]

Equity

Here follows a cautionary tale. Early-stage digital entrepreneurs need to think carefully about the equity of their businesses and the conditions which surround it. One of the most talented and successful UK digital entrepreneurs is Simon Nixon who founded MoneySupermarket.com, a website offering price comparison in financial services. MoneySupermarket floated successfully in August 2007 having enjoyed a spectacular eight-year growth rate. It was valued at £800m and Nixon was the majority shareholder.

Nixon had been interested in financial services for 20 years. Having dropped out of a financial accounting course at university in 1987, Nixon, then 20 years old, started out with a magazine aimed at mortgage brokers. Published fortnightly, it attempted to offer comprehensive rankings of every home loan on the market, enabling brokers to find the best deals for their clients much more quickly.

The business really took off two years later when Nixon first teamed up with Duncan Cameron, then an 18-year-old IT student and the brother of his then girlfriend. Cameron quit his course and the two men spent a year building a computerized version of the mortgage listings magazine that would enable brokers to compare products on a daily basis. That business, Mortgage 2000, grew steadily until 1999, when Nixon realized the potential of the internet for price comparison. The prospect of huge numbers of consumers suddenly getting access to the internet persuaded Nixon that millions of mortgage borrowers might represent a much more lucrative market than the relatively small community of professional mortgage advisers.

In 2002, Cameron departed the business but remained a 47% shareholder while Nixon took the strain. Reportedly, the two former business partners then stopped speaking to each other. Five years later, in 2007, with an IPO on the cards, Nixon needed Cameron out. He persuaded Cameron to sell the majority of his 47% stake in MoneySupermarket.com back to him for the not inconsiderable sum of £162m. A rueful Nixon is quoted as having said *'The worst deal I ever did was giving him half the business.'*[14]

The moral of the tale is clear. Do not give away equity (if you can avoid it) and, if you do, make sure that it reflects properly the recipients' contribution to the success of the business. Remember that, by giving away a percentage of the company, you are potentially giving away that percentage of the future profits of the company in perpetuity!

Entrepreneurs should thus consider the following:

- Try to avoid raising money unless you really have to and, if you do, consider carefully who to raise it from and how to prepare most effectively
- Make sure that you have proper planning processes with sensible budgets

- Understand the importance of cash
- Cash collection is a minefield: do not confuse your invoices with actual payment!
- Share options help to get staff members to think like owners rather than employees and this helps cash discipline
- Be fanatical about your cash control
- Exits are time-consuming and complicated: plan ahead!
- Take your time in hiring your professional advisers
- Do not give away equity unless you absolutely have to

Chapter Six

MARKETING

Marketing is too important to be left to the marketing department.

David Packard, co-founder of Hewlett Packard

In the 15 years since the internet got its commercial start, marketing has been transformed. This chapter will explain some of the most effective traffic drivers. The most important of these are viral marketing and the use of public relations, search engine optimization ('SEO'), pay-per-click ('PPC') and emails. There are other marketing channels which are still powerful, such as graphical advertising (namely, the banners and badges made popular in the early years of the internet, normally paid for on a 'cost per thousand impressions' (CPM) basis) and of course 'cost per acquisition' ((CPA) which is the cornerstone of the affiliate model). And in recent years, with the popularity of social networks, a whole new area of marketing has dawned utilizing websites such as Facebook and Twitter.

This chapter looks at a range of methods to drive traffic to your website. It describes how TV can work and how best to promote yourself virally. I explain some of the key levers by which you can maximize the number of visitors to your website by understanding how to appear in the search engine listings, how to maximize the effectiveness of PPC, and how to use social networks, email marketing and the affiliate model. Digital marketing allows even the smallest companies to compete with international giants. This chapter explains how.

A mongoose speaks

In 2009 an African mongoose transformed the fortunes of a British insurance price comparison website called comparethemarket. com. UK television had for long been crammed with commercials for price comparison websites, especially those that compared the cost of financial services. The reason for this was the lack of difference between these websites – so, unlike unique 'market-driving' websites, word-of-mouth would not do the trick. Then there was the simple fact that advertising for search terms (also called 'keywords') on Google for this category is very expensive (£5 for a search term like 'market' can be Google's going rate).

In this saturated market, comparethemarket was the smallest of the big four sites. Lacking a distinctive product and even a memorable name, it needed to do something dramatic to attract more users. So Aleksandr Orlov, possibly the oddest creature yet created in the history of the internet, hit the small screen.

Quite why a mongoose – or more precisely a meerkat – dressed as a Russian aristocrat in a smoking jacket and speaking with a thick foreign accent should capture the public's imagination quite so rapidly and completely is a bit of a mystery. But Aleksandr quickly established himself as a subject of dinner party conversation and one of the most influential characters on social media, the newest of all the internet's many marketing platforms.

At the time of writing, Aleksandr has over 600,000 Facebook fans and 25,000 Twitter followers. Aleksandr has his own website, 'comparethemeerkat.com', which is (naturally) the world's leading meerkat comparison website. This in itself has attracted over five million people comparing meerkats!

The conceit behind the campaign is that Aleksandr is irritated that a UK cheap car insurance price comparison website, comparethemarket.co.uk, which sounds so like his own meerkat website, comparethemeerkat.co.uk, is pulling away users who want to compare meerkats. So Aleksandr has launched an advertising campaign to clear up this market/meerkat confusion once and for all.

The results for comparethemarket were nothing less than phenomenal: its market share jumped by 76% while that of its rivals fell by some 32%, 25% and 5%. Admiral, a large insurance group and owner of one of comparethemarket.co.uk's competitors, Confused.com, cited Aleksandr when it revealed a 30% drop in operating profits for Confused.com.[1]

In the first five months of the campaign, comparethemarket.co.uk's traffic doubled and the cost per visit reduced by some 73%. Not surprisingly, its spontaneous brand awareness went up from fourth to first among the car insurance price comparison sites.[2]

The brilliance of the meerkat campaign, which was devised by London-based agency VCCP, was not just its originality. It was that it linked an offline campaign effectively with new media: in other words, the power of Google search as well as that of social media (Facebook, Twitter) to drive brand awareness. Not only that, but it kept the cost of its online search budget well down by cleverly using the cheaper keyword 'meerkat', at five pence, instead of the more expensive 'market' at £5.

The viral effect and public relations

Of course, if you do not have a truly differentiated product, then creative solutions such as Aleksandr can be a powerful driver of traffic to the website. And in the high margin and competitive world of financial services price comparison, TV has been the instrument of choice, with each brand vying for the amount of money it could pour into TV slots.

But there are many other ways apart from traditional advertising to drive traffic to websites. Traditional advertising is expensive (overspend on media was one of the key factors in the cash crisis faced by so many internet companies in 2000) and its impact can be hard to measure. Retailing tycoon John Wanamaker once said '*Half the money I spend on advertising is wasted; the trouble is I don't know which half.*'[3] That is a bit of an exaggeration. Nevertheless, the impact of online advertising is far easier to measure, and it is this that lies behind the success of Google and the continuing growth of online advertising generally.

The best possible way to drive traffic to websites, as seen in Chapter Three, is to be a market driving company. Aleksandr would still be enjoying his anonymity as a Moscow business meerkat had comparethemarket enjoyed a key differentiation from its online competitors. If you are a market driver the viral effect is fabulous. The internet is free. Most websites are free. So, unlike recommendations in the old economy, it is very easy for users to find out about a new website they like and then recommend those websites to a friend or family. Think about the websites that you use regularly: how many of them did you find out about from traditional media advertising, and how many by word of mouth? How did you hear about Google or Facebook or Twitter?

Imbuing a website with personality is, certainly, an excellent way to propel a viral effect, as Aleksandr has shown. But product distinctiveness is even more powerful. Google considered a multi-million dollar marketing budget in its early days, since in 1999 internet companies were spending big money on advertising in a race to win over users. Alta Vista, its main competitor, spent $120m on advertising in 1999. But Google decided not to opt for the big budget approach, instead focusing on word of mouth. That required a great deal of confidence in the quality of its product offering.[4]

eBay had a slightly different approach. It supplemented the originality of its idea (the global trading platform) with an invented story, namely that its founder had come up with the idea simply to help his fiancée trade PEZ dispensers, something that created a maelstrom of publicity.[5] The founder later admitted that this was an 'embellishment'.

Another company that used its story effectively was the online betting start-up Flutter.com. It was widely publicized that the idea for it had stemmed from the American founders' betting competitions during a Super Bowl party. This story was later dismissed by someone close to the company.[6]

Both Google and eBay discovered the power of the viral effect very early on. In each case, the product promoted with skilful PR proved a potent combination.

It is best to be truthful with journalists, and many internet companies do have interesting stories to tell without the need to embroider. Company founders can be hugely important in telling those stories. In the UK, Brent Hoberman and Martha Lane Fox were astute in explaining the virtues of booking online at the 'last minute', and embodied the heady excitement and 'make-it-happen' optimism of the early internet years. Craig Newmark's folksy community style has underscored the growth of his classified advertising website Craigslist. Amazon's Jeff Bezos is an accomplished showman. In 1999 he personally delivered an order of golf clubs to Amazon's 10 millionth customer, a man in Boston, while his most famous stunt is probably the tennis match he played with Anna Kournikova at Grand Central Terminal in New York in 2003 to publicize the tennis star's new range of sports bras available on Amazon ('only the ball should bounce').

Hatt certainly had an advantage when he founded Cheapflights as he had been a leading travel writer and therefore understood well how the press worked. One of the most impressive and memorable parts of the due diligence process on the sale of his company was the handing over of a huge pile of press cuttings books in which each and every press article had been lovingly pasted. It was another Hatt tradition that I maintained over the years as the cuttings book grew bigger and bigger.

Cheapflights always lent itself well to press coverage. There are endless stories around flying: not just the best deals available at any particular moment, but also trends (where is 'in' and where is not), airports (we once ran a very successful piece of research on the most child-friendly airports) and, of course, the airlines themselves (another story featured the most expensive airline gin and tonic). Cheaplights' analysis of legroom in economy class across different airlines proved especially popular.

mySupermarket.co.uk has used its shopping research too with good effect getting publicity for such stories as the 'vainest town in Britain' (the one which had the biggest spend on cosmetics), shrinking pack sizes (we pointed out examples where manufacturers were reducing their pack sizes and, in some cases, not cutting prices) and the reducing price of Easter eggs. The revelation that supermarkets had more promotions on 'alcopops' (a product consumed by young people) than any other type of alcohol received much coverage.

Obviously the best Cheapflights stories always related to new features on the website such as: a 'telephone cheat sheet' which gives you directions on how to 'speak to a human' at call centres in easy steps; a travel checklist for all the things you need to do before you leave home; and an analysis of the additional fees increasingly imposed by the airlines for, for example, baggage, fuel and choosing your seat. All these received wide exposure.

Our user surveys always provided a good source of publicity. We revealed that it is no longer bawling babies but drunks who are the people we would least like to find on board a plane. When we asked the question 'Which member of the British royal family would you like most or least to travel with?', again the results captured a great deal of attention. According to the poll results, Prince Philip (who has a bit of a history of making tactless remarks on his journeys) would be the worst royal to travel with followed by Camilla, Duchess of Cornwall, and Prince Edward, and the best royal as a travel companion would be Prince William.

Even a poll about the best freebies on flights got attention revealing that 19% of passengers believed the sick bag was the most grate-fully received giveaway. All these stories were connected with flying, demonstrated our rapport with the travelling public and helped to underscore our position as a consumer champion.

Not all our efforts were successful. When Heathrow Terminal Five opened, we sent a team to the terminal to celebrate the opening and, of course, to publicize the website. Little did the team know that inside the £4.3bn Terminal Five, chaos reigned as flights were cancelled, baggage was delayed and check-in came to a grinding halt. To add to passenger fury, none of the electronic announcement boards functioned either. It was amidst these scenes of anarchy and passenger anger that our enthusiastic and well-motivated PR task force arrived.

A better viral effort was Cheapflights' homage to '*Where the Hell is Matt?*', a YouTube video seen by about 15 million users. 'Matt' went around the world and managed to get himself captured on video performing a distinctive dance at some very recognizable locations. Our version showed 'Biggles' (Cheapflights' mascot bear) performing similar dances in some unexpected places including on the moon. It cost very little to make and itself got some 50,000 viewings.[7]

The Biggles bear was another example of bringing a bit of personality to a website. At travel trade conferences, we always had a large version of Biggles the Bear at our stands and often small ones (wearing a Cheapflights tee-shirt) as a giveaway. Without fail, the bears went like hot cakes. For a long time, the large bear would be comfortably seated in his own chair in the reception area of our London HQ.

It is also important to get out and talk about your digital business as often as you possibly can. Talking at conferences and trade shows is an important element of viral marketing. Happily, I have always enjoyed public speaking so this was not a great chore. One speaking engagement that I thought was going to be especially tricky was when I defended flying at London's 'Battle of Ideas', a weekend of debates on controversial issues arranged by the Institute of Ideas and sponsored by *The Times* newspaper, among others. As it turned out, there was a lot of support in the audience for cheap flights and we had a memorably lively question and answer session.

Another useful way to promote the viral effect is networking. Silicon Valley is certainly networking nirvana. But one of the advantages of London is that it too has a good digital network – so do not hide your light under a bushel. Go and tell opinion formers all about it.

One cheap and effective marketing method is the 'viral marketing' card. Just like an ordinary business card, it has only the logo and the website name upon it (no personal details). Give it out as often as you can: at restaurants to the waiting staff, to people at parties, to the person to whom you are chatting on the train. There are millions of websites, and if you think they will recall your domain name, even if you spell it out, you are kidding yourself. So hand out the card. People will be grateful for it.

Your online reputation

Be sure too to monitor your online reputation carefully. Viral marketing is a two-edged sword. The internet – with its blogs, social networks and rapid transmission of information – is not a one-way street which can be 'controlled'. 'Google Alerts' is a free way of tracking what is going on, although its coverage is not universal. There are a number of paid tracking services which are available in order to provide a fuller picture.

A major risk to any marketing effort is that adverse publicity or comment may appear in search results for your company or brand. So watch out for that and deal with it if and when it does happen. Respond positively and if the coverage is inaccurate, try to ensure that the commentator publishes a retraction. Failing that, make sure that your side of the story is heard fully.

Social networks now provide new platforms on which to share your story and manage your online reputation. Twitter, with its 140-character micro-blogging service, has now been embraced by businesses of all sorts. For any business, Twitter is just like any other brand presence: that is, it needs to support the brand value. If a tweeter from your company wants to express a personal opinion on something that is fine, but not under the company umbrella. Your Twitter style also should be in accordance with the principles of your brand. Most importantly, Twitter is not an old-fashioned broadcast channel. It is a network and that requires constant engagement with your followers. Some of the more digitally-aware airlines have used Twitter with great effect. Among these is JetBlue, which provides an object lesson on how to use this new medium to the full dealing promptly with customer complaints and keeping its passengers up to date with relevant travel news. At the time of writing, JetBlue has 1.6 million followers.

Search engine optimization (SEO)

When you search for something on Google or, for that matter, on any search engine, the order of the results that come up is not an accident. The results are organized into two sections. The first items on the list, as well as the ones in the right-hand column, are paid for. ('Paid-for' search is covered later in this chapter.) The rest are called 'natural' (or 'organic' or 'free') search results, and they are *not* paid for.

Google and its rivals are constantly trying to ensure that search results are as relevant as possible. They do this using technology such as, in Google's case, PageRank (see Chapter One). As a business, you can influence this process to increase the flow of traffic to your website. You do this by improving how highly you are ranked by the search engine's 'relevance' technology. This activity is called 'search engine optimisation' ('SEO'), or 'natural search'. Every company online needs to think carefully about how to get a high ranking on as many as possible of the free (natural) search results.

The aim of SEO is, proactively, to draw into your website users who don't know about you, but who are searching in your general area of goods or services with search terms or keywords, e.g. cars, washing machines, theatre tickets, chiropodists.

It is worth noting that, aside from the traffic you draw in through your skills in SEO, you will also get traffic from the search engines (that you do not pay for) as a result of users entering your company name as a search term when they either do not know your exact web address, or can't be bothered to type it out in full in the browser. This is called 'navigational search'.

'Natural search' always contains a component of 'navigational search', which, incidentally, usually allows for spelling mistakes. (Google does this by means of a prompter so that if, for example, you entered '*Chepflits*', the prompter will ask '*Did you mean "Cheapflights"?*') So part of any successful SEO or 'natural search' strategy is building your brand awareness so that users will type your brand into Google's search field. This alone will boost the traffic you get from the search engine.

Brands themselves are now significant search terms. For instance, while Thomas Cook is by no means the most popular travel agency website, it ranks as the most popular search term within the travel agency category simply because it is such a well-known brand.[8] But there are also many other ways apart from brand recognition by which you can improve the likelihood of being found and prioritized in search results.

SEO is a complex business; but given the huge usage of search (and especially Google's dominance: it accounts for over 70% of the search market in the USA and over 80% in the UK), it is worth investing time, effort and money in it. Between 50 and 70% of search engines' users click onto websites listed in the free section of the results. So, with no direct cost, it can transform the profitability of a company.[9]

Because SEO is hard, many websites try easier options such as traditional offline advertising and PPC (see below). It is much easier to, say, festoon London buses with some brightly coloured ads or to commit a budget to Google AdWords than it is to work out how to enter and stay at the top of the free search rankings.

Internet businesses therefore have a choice: either decide to commit to SEO properly, dedicating to it the necessary time and effort, and enjoying the huge rewards if successful; or forget it and focus on other marketing channels. It might require you to alter the design of your website significantly. Implementing just one or two changes and expecting them to propel your website into a top Google position won't work.

'Reputation' is critical to successful SEO strategies. It is calculated by various factors. The most important is the number of users coming to your website having clicked on a link from another website – 'inbound' links – and the reputation of the website they have come from. Reputation is based on a social networking principle. Inbound links are regarded as 'votes'. The higher the reputation of the website they have clicked from, the better your website's reputation becomes; a sort of halo effect. This is commonly known as 'PageRank', the result of the algorithm developed by Larry Page and Sergey Brin (see Chapter One).

Reputation is also heightened if the site that users come from is closely related to your own, e.g. for a travel website, an inbound link from another travel website is worth more than one from a general online directory. It is similar to an 'expert opinion' as they are both in the same field. In other words, if someone who critiques this book has a distinguished background in digital commerce (for example, Eric Schmidt), the weight of that opinion is greater than that of, say, a renowned ski instructor. But if this book was about the most challenging ski pistes in Switzerland, then the view of the instructor might outweigh that of the digital business person (even Eric Schmidt).

Reputation-building is absolutely key for any online business that wants to perform well in free, natural search results. It is important not only to maintain a website's existing 'votes', but also to continue to build them. It is vital to ensure that your website has great and relevant content to which people want to link and that any mention of your website or company on a third party website has a link to yours. So, for example, if an online magazine writes an article about your website and mentions its name, be sure that it includes a clickable link. Continue to raise your website's online brand awareness, for instance through press releases and the blogosphere.

If you are in the design stage of your website, consider carefully its internal structure. This is commonly an afterthought by major sites but it should be at the heart of the website design. Search engine robots (or 'bots') trawl through a website trying to accumulate as much information as possible to improve the validity of their results. They keep a copy of this information in their database to provide search results to their users by matching their query to the information in their own database.

The structure of a website is therefore important to a search engine. Essentially, information on pages closest to the home page are deemed more important than items deeply hidden several clicks away. A good analogy is a shop front. A large department store like Selfridges spends thousands of pounds on displaying its best products prominently to lure customers. It would not hide its best products in a back storeroom. Well-optimized websites (that is, websites that are constructed so that they will be found by the search engine robots) will often display their most market-competitive/highest revenue-generating products on their home page. By raising the profile of these products on the website, they are highlighting their importance to search engines.

Consider carefully the content on your website. The old cliché 'content is king' is still valid today. Websites with large amounts of good content will perform better with search engines than sites with little or no content for the 'bots' to latch onto. TripAdvisor is a classic example of an internet business which has a sophisticated grasp of SEO. It uses user-generated content not only to enhance its own website *per se*, but also to ensure that the page is found by the search engines. TripAdvisor's strength in SEO ensures that it is in the top-ranked results for very popular search terms like 'hotels in New York/London/Paris' as well as of course the long tail of less frequently searched terms such as 'hotels in Clovis/ Rapid City'.

Pay strict attention to your HTML page titles (the titles that appear at the very top of your browser) as they are a primary index for search engines. As titles are a feature of the browser, and not the web page itself, page designers don't see them. So quite often website owners will pay little attention to them, not realizing that they will appear in search engine results and that they are a key factor for good optimization. Titles should accurately and succinctly describe what the page is about using words that are commonly searched for and appear on the page.

A well-constructed document will contain a title and headings: a web page is the same. So utilizing 'header tags' appropriately is also very important. In most instances, the first heading on a web page should mirror the HTML page title in the browser, enforcing the page's relevance to a target search term.

Descriptions too should be created with the utmost care. This is a direct marketing opportunity and, as such, you should be sure to maximize their potential, ensuring succinctness, accuracy and relevance.

It is core to your SEO success to have a keyword strategy. This will focus on the search terms that your online business is targeting. If you are setting up a website to sell something, you will want to ensure that you cover all the potential associated keywords. Sometimes these are not at all obvious. Happily, these are established by third party sources (e.g. Hitwise) and you can look them up. You can also use your own website analytics. But use commonsense: there was a time when both 'Jordan' and 'Paris Hilton' looked like top search terms for travel, but sadly searchers were looking neither for Petra nor the Eiffel Tower – or even for cheap flights!

Keyword density is another important measure. This is a percentage measurement of the occurrences of your target keyword phrase on a page as a percentage of all of its content. The higher the occurrence of your page's targeted keywords, the more 'relevant' your page is to that term for the bots. However, you do need to monitor carefully what is 'normal' in your particular business. If you are optimizing to a keyword density of 5%, and all of your competition is optimizing to 1–2%, you may be flagged and penalized for 'overoptimization'. It is therefore very important to measure not only your own site's keyword density but also that of your competitors.

Once your keyword strategy is defined, it becomes important to test how well you are doing, tracking how often your website comes up – and how high in the ranking – when your keywords are used in searches. Fluctuations of search results are completely natural and should not give cause for alarm. The key is to measure your overall visibility across a wide array of search terms. When I was running Cheapflights, I had around 20 terms (which I picked at random from our keyword strategy list) on which I checked every few days to ensure that we were at the top of our game.

Bear in mind too that SEO has become so crucial that many businesses try to fool the search engines into believing that they have relevant content. In travel, there are scores of websites that indulge in 'black hat' SEO marketing. They build a seemingly unrelated series of websites, which are in fact based on the same content, that link to each other to boost rankings. Black hat SEO marketing can be very lucrative as it short-cuts the need to build a huge library of content, links and relevance.

Short term it can attract big traffic. However, it is also a very risky technique. When Google finds sites involved in black hat techniques, it typically responds quickly and mercilessly by cutting off the sites involved. In contrast, the rankings maintained by leading brands such as TripAdvisor and Cheapflights are 'white hat' SEO marketing as they are maintained by the unique, genuine and 'independent' nature of the content.[10]

In 2009, an independent UK search marketing agency announced the results of its analysis of 77 million Google flight-related search results. It used this data to rank the most visible brands on page one of Google's 'natural search' results. During May 2009, it concluded that Cheapflights.co.uk led the field with 92% visibility, its nearest competitors trailing with 64% and 42%, respectively. It commented '*Cheapflights.co.uk takes pole position when looking specifically at domestic, short haul and long haul destination keywords.*'[11]

So, who should be responsible for your SEO activity? Like every aspect of the internet business, one key question to resolve is getting the balance right between in-house versus external support for your SEO role. It is my solid belief that the best answer even for a smaller business is, as soon as the business is able practically to afford one, to recruit an online marketer with good background in SEO, supported by a good external agency. This ensures that SEO is ingrained within a business's day-to-day operation and not regarded as an afterthought. In this ultra-competitive environment, this is crucial and ensures the company is getting the best out of its appointed search agency. Typically at Cheapflights, during agency beauty parades, we would set far more store by an agency that brought in their best SEO expert for the pitch rather than their best sales executive.

Finally, a salutary tale to demonstrate why even an excellent search strategy alone is not adequate to guarantee your continuing success. In respect of their 'free' listings, the search engines have no relationships with third party websites. In his best-selling account of Google, John Battelle tells the sad story of Neil Moncrief, who co-founded a specialist website called 2bigfeet.com in 1999. This was the ultimate specialist e-commerce operation, specializing in the sale of large shoes (size 13 and up) – a perfectly logical idea, as large-footed people are geographically dispersed and therefore a bricks-and-mortar outlet will tend to be a bit empty for most of the time. Moncrief's website was certainly relevant and, as such, his key search terms (such as 'big feet') drove ever-increasing amounts of customers to his business.

But in November 2003, Moncrief's website slipped off the Google rankings and the business ground to a halt. Four thousand pairs of very large shoes with no buyers. What had happened was that Google had launched a concerted effort against black hat practices, and poor Moncrief got washed away in the tsunami that followed. All his key terms fell from the first page of the Google rankings to the fiftieth. Few users actually get to the fiftieth page of Google (you might as well be on page 100,000). He was not a spammer; he was not a black hatter. He was just a chap selling shoes. But his business crumbled. He immediately purchased AdWords to make up for some of the lost demand (and that would have reduced his margins) and, after about eight months, with some changes to his website, he worked his way back up to the top of the Google rankings.[12]

Moral: do not rely on free search alone.

Pay-per-click

One way to balance reliance on free search is to use paid-for search, or pay-per-click ('PPC'). As referred to in the previous section, these are the ranked advertising entries featured at the very top and down the side of search results pages.

PPC offers another way to get users to visit your site, in this case by their clicking on an online advertisement that you place on a third party website. Each time a user 'clicks through' to your website you make a payment to the third party.

PPC is popular with advertisers since, as the advertiser only pays when a user clicks through to their site, it not only is highly measurable but can be very cost-effective. In addition, since users choose to click on the link to your site, they are 'high quality' leads (by clicking, they have demonstrated they are genuinely interested in the content of your advertisement). So, although there is no guarantee any business will result from a given click-through lead, there is a much higher likelihood of this happening, per pound or dollar spent, than is the case with many forms of traditional advertising.

By far the biggest PPC platforms are the search engines. There, the positions on search results pages reserved for PPC are available to anyone wanting to advertise – for a price. Advertisers clearly want to secure those highly visible and relevant slots. This is achieved by bidding in a continuous auction process for the right for your advertisement to appear there every time a particular search term is used. The 'bid' is for the amount you are willing to pay each time a user clicks on your advertisement.

But in this process there is another element, which is how skilful you are at creating online advertisements that attract clicks by users. If your advertisement is well constructed, then it will draw a lot of 'click-through' (demonstrating a high level of 'relevance' to the search term used); you get the traffic, the third party gets their 'per-click payment' and the user, hopefully, finds what he or she is searching for. Everyone is happy. If the advertisement is weak, however, and users don't click through, then you will be penalized by being dropped down the rankings. So the quality of your advertisement, and its relevance, are crucial.

How you get to appear in the PPC platform rankings, therefore, is a blend of factors.

PPC platforms were developed in the USA (see Chapter One). The first was called GoTo (see page 19), and allowed advertisers simply to bid for keywords on their search engine. So, whenever a user entered that keyword into the search box, the advertiser's text would automatically come up. GoTo launched in the UK in 2000. The other early PPC platform available in the UK was the British company Espotting. These were the two service providers with whom I worked when managing Cheapflights' PPC activity in the early days. Then, in 2002, Google launched AdWords in the UK.[13]

Nowadays Google dominates PPC advertising; but its arch-rival Microsoft has recently launched Bing in order to compete more effectively.

PPC has grown in sophistication over the years and can be just as complex as SEO. It requires both investment and, most importantly, a lot of patience. As the internet has mushroomed, demand for these paid-for slots on search engine results pages has increased dramatically. It has become much more difficult managing a company's PPC activities, given the number of possible keywords, the increasing number of advertisers vying for available slots, and the inevitable trade-off calculation you therefore have to make about how many, and which, keywords you want to bid for, and at what price. And this is a constantly moving market. Additionally, it requires well-honed verbal and presentational skills since the precise content of your advertisement can influence whether or not users click on it rather than on your competitor's entry.

At a certain level of PPC spend you will need a 'bid optimization' (also called a 'bid management') platform. This will automatically adjust bids to produce the maximum amount of traffic in order to achieve your target return on investment. PPC bid management platforms are usually billed on a monthly retainer plus a percentage of spend. So it's all about economies of scale. If you have small spend levels, then the additional benefit gained from using a bid management tool may not offset the additional cost of the platform.

Bid optimization platforms have their advantages and disadvantages. For example, they react a lot more quickly than humans, updating bids multiple times a day, and in near real time (usually a three hour delay). However, they need to be properly set up and managed, and can be quite costly in terms of initial implementation, monthly fees and ongoing support. You can get into difficulties if a keyword you have bid for is not successful, leading to a reduction in the price you can afford to bid, in turn resulting in your entry falling down in the rankings – leading to even less visibility, and so on in a downward spiral.

As we will see later, to maximize your reach you can use more than one PPC provider. Any small business needs to consider carefully which, and how many, platforms are right for it. This adds an additional layer of complexity, but a good bid management system can handle this. There are lots of different PPC bid management solutions on the market, ranging from managed services, where an agency takes care of everything, to a software tool that runs on your desktop.

A bid optimization platform, however, is only as powerful as its operator. It cannot make correct keyword selection, nor can it compile good advertising copy – and, as we have seen, getting the wording right in your advertisements is a vital factor in PPC marketing success.

The key measure to assess the effectiveness of a PPC campaign is the 'click-through rate' or CTR. The higher the CTR, the better, and having good CTR rates will help reduce your cost per click as Google, for instance, takes this into account when calculating rankings. It is impossible to generalize as to what a good click-through rate is. It depends on the profit you make from the click and the cost of that click. Ideally you will want to make money from your PPC investment that is having a high click-through rate compared with others on a search term and by making more money from the visit to your website than the cost of that lead.

So how do you improve your CTR and thus demonstrate your good online advertising abilities? This is a skilled area. For example, you have a very limited word count allowance in which to get the unique points about your product or service across, and you need a title that stands out and grabs the user's attention. But you must be careful not to overpromise. If users click on your advertisement but are then disappointed with what they find, they will click back (typically referred to as a 'bounce rate' or 'single page click'). This is click-through money wasted for the advertiser.

An example of a well-thought-through and compelling creative is an advertisement from British car insurance price comparison site GoCompare.com:

> *You could save £212 in 5 minutes by comparing 110+ car insurers with us*
>
> *GoCompare.com*

It sets out a tangible benefit, and quantified cost and time savings, and indicates access to a wide breadth of insurance suppliers, all in one very short sentence.

As I mentioned earlier, good keyword strategy is the heart of any effective search strategy. It is critical to understand what terms your users enter into search engines. Keyword research may reveal that what you believe users will use may be very different from what they actually use, and you will no doubt find keyword patterns that had not originally occurred to you. You need to build a keyword universe of search terms you know 'convert' for you. There are several sources of keyword data online, for instance Google AdWords, WordTracker, WordStream and Experian Hitwise. Also the 'Google AdWords Traffic Estimator'[14] shows you what you can expect to pay for different keywords.

One word of caution about keywords: there's an important legal issue now under consideration. For some years now a battle has been raging around the world between brand owners on the one side and search engine operators (and their keyword customers) on the other side on the following question: does the unauthorized use of keywords for the purpose of internet advertising infringe third party registered trade marks to which they are identical or confusingly similar? In other words, if I am selling books online, I should not attempt to buy keywords like Amazen and Amazan to draw people to my website. Trying this might result in finding yourself at the wrong end of an infringement suit.

To ensure maximum reach, use keyword analytics (the systems which inform you what words people search for when they come to your site, so 'flights' might be an important one for Cheapflights) to understand which keywords users use to come to your site via free search, and then make sure you also have visibility with these same keywords in the paid-for areas. But, you might ask, if users come in via *free* search, why *pay* for them with PPC as well?

The answer is that not everyone who goes to search engines clicks on the free listings. Many users will click on the first thing they see and, if that is a paid listing and you are not present in that section, you could be losing potential users and revenue. Search engines will emphasize paid listings as they are such a crucial revenue source. They will also syndicate their paid-for search results to other companies. All good additional reasons to give PPC serious consideration.

The danger of PPC is, of course, overspend. It can be like a drug. Businesses can get very hooked on it as the traffic pours in, especially if they do not have a clear idea of how profitable it really is. You need to set your own rules about what you expect from your paid campaigns – for example, that all PPC spend has to produce a return of at least 20%. And, as for SEO, make sure that you do not have all your advertising eggs in one PPC basket. Use a variety of advertising channels.

To do this effectively, tracking is key. Without proper tracking, you are flying blind. You need to understand fully, for each and every one of those paid leads, what they have done on your site and how effectively you have monetized them. Margins differ hugely across industry sectors. So, for example, gambling or financial services will be able to bid high rates for click-through leads (just remember the £5 cost for 'market' which persuaded Comparethemarket.com to opt for the more affordable 'meerkat' instead). In the travel sector margins are significantly less, so PPC rates are much lower.

With Google dominating the UK search market, why bother with other search platforms? If you are already reaping a positive return on investment from your Google account but want to increase traffic and/or profitability further, then it does make sense to diversify traffic sources. Depending on the industry sector of your online business, Yahoo and/or Bing traffic may have a better conversion rate than Google's.

So, who should look after your PPC activities? For a small business, an experienced internal resource is fine. For major internet sites, however, a mixture of both internal and external resources is important. Today's bidding environment is far from simple and it is worth enlisting the help of a digital marketing agency to help set up and run your account.

The affiliate model

The so-called affiliate model provides purchase opportunities wherever people may be surfing. It does this by offering financial incentives (in the form of a percentage of revenue) to affiliated partner sites. The affiliates provide purchase-point click-through to the merchant. It is a pay-for-performance model. If an affiliate does not generate sales, it represents no cost to the merchant. The affiliate model is inherently well suited to the web, which explains its huge popularity. The affiliate model has, for example, served Amazon very well. In the early days of Cheapflights we used to link into Amazon's travel books. We did not sell many. But it was gratifying at that time of an early stage business to get even small amounts regularly trickling in for little effort on our part. With a simple log-in, I could see what books we had sold and what our commission was.

Using social networks

Malmö is Sweden's third biggest city and is a place well known to readers of Henning Mankell's best-selling *Wallander* detective books. Malmö is also the location for a new IKEA store – and not just any new IKEA store but one which has used social media with extraordinary effectiveness. Market-driving IKEA was quick to realise the importance of digital media to spread the word. It engaged an advertising agency called Forsman and Bodenfors to create a very special launch campaign that used Facebook as its platform.

During late 2009, the agency created a Facebook profile for the store manager, one Gordon Gustavsson. Then, over a two-week period, it uploaded 12 images of various displays from the IKEA showrooms to his photo album. Understanding fully the widespread reach of Facebook as well as the popularity of its tagging feature, it put out the word that the person who first tagged a particular product could win it.

The demand for more IKEA pictures quickly grew. Swedes, ravenous for free IKEA items, asked for more images so that they too could tag something, anything – a chair, a picture, a set of cutlery. The pictures spread to tens of thousands of Facebook users via their profile pages, the newsfeed and links.

This was new media at its most dynamic. In the old days, it might have been a one-page advertisement in the Malmö newspaper or catalogues delivered expensively door-to-door. Now, instead of getting potential buyers passively to look at advertisements or catalogues, IKEA skilfully managed to persuade Facebook users personally to promote their merchandise, spinning out the word speedily and on a huge scale, using the familiar Facebook functionality. It was a huge marketing success.

If you cannot afford a cutting-edge marketing agency to advise you on how effectively to use Facebook, do not despair. At the very least, avail yourself of Facebook's free tools to market your business. 'Fan pages' are, for instance, an excellent way to stimulate interest and to build up loyalty.

Twitter too has been discovered by businesses large and small as a potent marketing platform. Dell claimed by the end of 2008 already to have earned some $1m in computer sales through alerts posted on the micro-blogging site[15] – and that was before Twitter really took off as a global phenomenon. By the end of 2009, ComScore was estimating Twitter's global traffic at 60 million visitors a month. No wonder that even small businesses were becoming aware of its potential. San Francisco corner café Mission Pie is one such business. Its Twitter followers now number over 1,000. Business is brisk, and its co-owner gives some of the credit to Twitter: '*It has a lot of street credibility that's not there with traditional media.*'[16]

Email marketing

Remember that time when you could hardly open your front door because of the huge volumes of direct mail that landed on your mat, envelopes full of glossy brochures and enticing offers? Well, email has for long been providing a modern-day substitute. As many people consider unsolicited advertising mail (of the 'e' as well as paper variety) a profound nuisance, anyone contemplating launching an internet business needs to think about how best to use email.

In the middle of a deep recession, email marketing is witnessing rapid growth. In 2009 it rose by an estimated 15%.[17]

Cheapflights launched its first email campaigns over 10 years ago. Not only was it a useful way of reinforcing the brand, it was highly effective in encouraging repeat visits. By promoting compelling flight deals we were able to attract users back into the website, perhaps at times when they would not ordinarily have been considering travel. By using emails, websites can 'push' their message to their audiences. This contrasts with search engines, where you rely on someone searching, or website-based advertising, which also relies on the customer to be proactive in visiting the website.

One of the most compelling reasons to use email marketing is its low cost, certainly compared with its old economy predecessors, namely direct mail and printed newsletters. And the costs of email marketing and measuring the effectiveness of emails are rapidly reducing, which is good news especially for smaller enterprises.

Just as with SEO and PPC, emailed newsletters are very measurable: you can see what the 'open rate' is (how many people open the email), what the 'bounce rate' is (showing out-of-date addresses) and what the click rate on the newsletter itself is. Of course, the more targeted you make your emails the better the results, and the less likely you are to annoy people with irrelevant clutter in their inbox. For example, if you are sending out flight deals, you can attain higher open rates and clicks if you can identify and email appropriately to, for example, skiers, or those who prefer beach holidays.

Always ensure that your emails are 'opt in'. Spam (named apparently after the famous Monty Python sketch in which the word 'spam' is repeatedly sung)[18] is one of the major bugbears of the internet. It is the modern version of junk mail, and PC software customarily has spam or junk mail filters to get rid of it. There is a huge difference between a user receiving an opted-in email – potentially useful – and an unsolicited one, which is mere spam (and usually useless).

Every time you send out an email, use it as an opportunity to test what is working. Just as good sales people know what 'ABC' stands for ('always be closing'), so the best email marketers know 'ABT' – 'always be testing'.

If anyone doubts the effectiveness of email, then they should talk to Thomas Gensemer of Blue State Digital. It was Gensemer who masterminded Democratic candidate Barack Obama's 2008 email campaign: he amassed a 13.4 million email list (20% of American voters), segmented it into 300 'tracks', sent out 2 billion email messages, and raised over $500m. Using emails, he even persuaded farmers to paint their buildings in a 'Barns for Obama' campaign.

Anyone want a pixel?

The internet has been a liberator for entrepreneurs. To get famous you do not need to possess the budget of Coca-Cola or Nike. This power of the internet to launch a business cheaply and then reach a huge public is demonstrated by Milliondollarhomepage. com in 2005. Eschewing every traditional type of internet market-ing device (he had no money for this), its 21-year-old British founder Alex Tew made an initial investment of £50 on the domain name and a basic web-hosting package. Then, he proceeded to sell a pixel on his page for one dollar.

The idea was simple: to try to make $1m by selling 1,000,000 pixels (hence, 'The Million Dollar Homepage'). As Alex said: '*The main motivation for doing this is to pay for my degree studies, because I don't like the idea of graduating with a huge student debt. I know people who are paying off student loans 15–20 years after they graduated. Not a nice thought!'* Alex sold $1,000 worth of pixels by word of mouth, and then sent out a press release which was picked up by the BBC. The rest of the world's press soon took up the story. Pixelmania became rampant. Even Cheapflights bought sufficient pixels for our logo to be seen on this then-famous digital canvas. Just before reaching his target of a million dollars, requests for orders were being received at a rate of 100,000 pixels per hour, so Tew decided to hold back the last 1,000 and put them up for auction on eBay. They fetched $38,000.[19]

Before the internet, marketing was expensive. Scaling a business took time and resources. Big brands dominated hugely expensive traditional media. Now a small internet company can make its presence known if it is agile and remains on top of the various levers necessary to pull to get improved traffic.

In summary:

- The internet is a very 'viral' medium. Word of mouth means that internet sites can gain traction very quickly but skilful use of advertising and public relations can help accelerate that take-up
- Search engine optimization is complex and requires a constant investment of time: the work needed to maintain high rankings in the search engines is never complete but it is an important part of keeping your website more visible than that of your competitors
- PPC is similarly complex. Make sure that you understand fully the costs and revenues associated with your campaigns

- The rise and rise of social networks means that they are already becoming an important source of traffic; so get to understand them well to maximize their potential
- Email marketing is the new direct mail but is far cheaper and far easier to analyse. Use email to push relevant people to your website but avoid spamming at all costs
- The affiliate model can be very attractive. You can increase your exposure and make money
- Alex Tew demonstrated one of the basic truths of the internet. You do not need a lot of money to get a following. With an intriguing idea and some skilful PR, Tew made a million dollars.

Chapter Seven

THE REST
OF THE WORLD

*The World is a book, and those who do not travel read only
a page.*

St Augustine of Hippo

If you succeed in your domestic market, especially if your market
is as small as that of the UK, inevitably your thoughts will turn at
some stage to overseas expansion. This chapter offers my obser-
vations on how best to do this, partly based on my own experience
of seeing Cheapflights launched in the USA, but also on watching
the successes and failures of other international strategies.

Global expansion is anything but straightforward despite the huge
opportunities that the internet has brought. Even the apparently
welcoming USA is not as straightforward a market to crack as some
may imagine. Europe has its own set of complications and each
country needs to be tackled differently. Both Japan and China,
though vast in scale, are also vast in complexity. I am not seeking
to describe every internet market in the world. There are undoubtedly opportunities from Armenia to Zambia; but I am trying to
draw generic lessons from some of the world's larger and more
mature internet markets.

At worst folly

The head of the newly-appointed PR agency for Cheapflights USA looked serious when Hugo Burge and I entered the conference room. On the previous day, one of the travel journalists had reacted badly to his pitch, not fully understanding Cheapflights' consumer proposition. The PR man announced that the website just wouldn't work in the USA and that American travellers wouldn't get it. Hugo and I remained silent, dismayed by this singular lack of enthusiasm. Then the PR man added, with a flourish, that Prêt-a-Manger (the British sandwich shop chain) had found the American market very difficult.

The PR man was not alone. Long before we decided on an American launch for Cheapflights some of our investors had expressed grave reservations. No British internet company had succeeded in the American market. The internet industry was an American-devised industry and American companies were coming to Europe in their droves. For a British internet company to raise the Union Jack on American soil seemed at best overambitious, and at worst folly.

Over the years the USA has indeed proved a graveyard for British companies. One famous UK company, GEC (later renamed Marconi), bought an American internet switching company in 1999 called Fore Systems for $4.5bn. It proved to be Marconi's undoing. Within four years, the 100-year-old company, once one of the UK's largest with a stock market value of £35bn, was no more. Similarly, outside tech, British failure to crack the American market was legendary. As a poignant reminder of how even the best British companies can get things horribly wrong, in November 2001, retailing giant Marks & Spencer sold Brooks Brothers for $225m. It had bought the famous clothes chain 13 years before for $750m!

So if mega-corps, the cream of the British business establishment like GEC/Marconi or Marks & Spencer, could mess up in the USA, what hope had a small start-up?

But ours was not as rash a move as some thought. First and foremost our business model was unique. And it had been tried and tested by UK consumers for seven years. The UK at that time (2003) was the home of cheap flights. Cheap flights were to British consumers what hamburgers and hot dogs were to Americans. In the USA, the 'legacy carriers' (the traditional airlines) had maintained a vice-like grip over the industry. Those few charter airlines that had tried to enter the market were squashed. Southwest Airlines had demonstrated the success of the low-cost model, but the legacy carriers ignored it as some sort of regional aberration, a quirky one-off outfit that did not merit too much attention.

In Britain things were very different. A vibrant charter flight market had grown up since the 1950s, offering heavily-discounted fares and often including accommodation in 'package deals'. The dreary weather in the UK meant that millions were soon escaping the rain-soaked beaches of Blackpool and Clacton for the sunnier climes of Spain, Greece and other warm destinations. And they were escaping by the only practical means of transport available: air.

By the 1990s, in a newly-prosperous Britain, a new form of airline travel started: the no-frills carriers. Unlike the USA where Southwest Airlines went from strength to strength, with no one else mimicking their cheap fares, use of secondary airports, unallocated seating and absence of business class, in the UK several low-cost carriers competed for custom. Stelios Haji-Ioannou's easyJet and the Irish Ryanair led the way. Soon British Airways launched its own low-cost carrier Go, and KLM similarly launched Buzz. So British consumers, by the late 1990s, were overwhelmed with choice in a vicious airline price war that has lasted to this day. This was the flying public that was using Cheapflights to help it identify the best flight deals.

In America, land of competition, the flights market was, well, rather less competitive. But that was going to change. The arrival of the internet and the early launches of online travel agencies Expedia and Travelocity meant that consumers were able to do a little bit of shopping around themselves. JetBlue, a serious low-cost carrier, launched its operations in 2000. And after the tragedy of 9/11, the American airlines had to do something to fill up their empty planes and began aggressively using price as a weapon.

Like British Airways and KLM, some American carriers even introduced their own low-cost efforts, for example United's Ted and Delta's Song. This inevitably led to enhanced consumer choice and massive fare discounting, an ideal environment in which Cheapflights could launch.

So by 2002, with UK traffic exceeding 1 million unique users a month for the first time, we decided to launch in the USA and in May 2003 our US website, Cheapflights.com, went live for the first time. Now, seven years later, our North American business (we have a Canadian operation too, Cheapflights.ca, launched in April 2007) accounts for over half our activities and remains both growing and profitable. While Cheapflights started in London and is proud of its British heritage, it is today flourishing on both sides of the Atlantic. Not very many British or even European consumer-facing websites have achieved this. Moreover since the launches in the USA and Canada, Cheapflights has started German, Australian/ New Zealand, Spanish and French businesses with more countries planned.

Here are my 10 top tips (in no particular order) for any entrepreneur thinking about expanding into the USA.

1. Do your homework

Naturally, if Cheapflights was to build a global business then a presence in the USA was a necessity. It is hard to imagine a global internet business which is not present there. But in several respects it was an odd choice. It is the most competitive internet market in the world with a very demanding user base. Its travel habits are very different from Europe's. Americans do precious little leisure travelling relative to Europeans. And most of their air travel is domestic. The obvious overseas market for Cheapflights to enter was Germany which has remarkably similar characteristics to those of Britain: unpredictable climate and a population with a predilection for sunny spots abroad – and lots of leisure time. At one time the Germans were said to spend more money on foreign holidays than on oil which, since Germany has the fourth-biggest economy in the world and do not produce one litre of their own oil, is saying something.

My main concern was that, as the concept of cheap flights took hold in post-9/11 America, an American internet business would try to reproduce what we did in their much bigger (five times the size) market and then come to the UK and swamp us. So it was important to ensure that did not happen.

So we did some extensive due diligence. First, we analysed the various travel price comparison companies that had launched in the USA and satisfied ourselves that no one had anything like our model – or were anywhere close to building one. As importantly, we talked to our major clients in the UK who had large US businesses, such as British Airways and Travelocity. They not only said they would put their deals on our site, but they urged us to break into the USA as soon as possible so that we could provide them with the converting leads. That was welcome news. It meant not only that some heavy-duty players in our industry believed that our website would work in the USA but also that from the day of the launch we would have paying customers. On the day of the launch we displayed 400 destinations, 200 departure points and 100,000 prices. Both British Airways and Travelocity were as good as their word and displayed their deals.

2. Go native

Cheapflights is a British company with British investors. When we launched in the USA, we did not have a single American on the payroll. This worried me. It seemed to me that as a British company trading in the USA for the first time, we had to get fully absorbed into the American business community. The key challenges therefore were to make sure that American opinion formers understood our proposition and were willing to endorse us – and that meant first-rank PR. Second, we needed to become part and parcel of the American online travel community. And third, we needed to access the wealth of technology talent available locally. We had to become, as rapidly as possible, Americanized and accepted as a serious player in both the American digital and travel scene.

PR has always been an important part of Cheapflights' corporate armoury and is a necessity for a market-driving company, especially one with no budget for advertising. We parted ways with our first PR company, the one which did not share our vision and which likened us to the British sandwich chain Prêt-a-Manger. Whatever issues Prêt-a-Manger were then having in New York (and by the way, whenever I am in Manhattan I keep seeing their outlets), it seemed to me an ill-judged comparison. So we set about finding another agency.

After talking to several journalists and seeking their recommendations, we found a feisty and energetic firm based in New York, the sort of outfit that would not take 'no' from a journalist. They even managed to persuade the original bruising journalist that we were onto something. That journalist had provided us with some very useful comments, some of which we subsequently adopted on the website. For example, he hated our 'A–Z' navigation system (click on 'P' if you want to go to Phoenix) and said we should adopt the industry norm of a search box. From the original pummelling from that one irascible travel journalist, we began to get a very positive response.

The US travel industry has a major 'must attend' digital event every year called PhocusWright for everyone involved in online travel. The driving spirit behind PhocusWright is Philip Wolf, its CEO, who runs one of the best conferences I have attended, either in travel or in any other industry. Hugo and I met Philip soon after starting at Cheapflights when we attended a European version of his conference in Montreux, Switzerland, in 2000. We decided that to gain industry knowledge alone it was worth travelling to the US main event later that year. Not only did we gather industry knowledge, but we also got to know Philip and his team which again proved invaluable when we finally did launch. When we were still quite new in the USA, Philip offered us an on-stage appearance, which we took up with relish.

To link into the digerati, I suggested that we approach Dan Bricklin, the co-creator of Visicalc, the pioneering financial spreadsheet whom I had known since we were in the same MBA class over 20 years before. I reckoned that we had something that Dan would like: a very easy and fast consumer interface that you could not find anywhere else, where a morass of complex and changing data was automatically sorted into clear results. Dan is the very model of a computer legend. If he, a fully paid-up member of America's digitocracy, liked the Cheapflights model, I believed that we would make the breakthrough.

So I approached him with a view to his joining our US board and he agreed to talk. It turned out that he was going to New York from Boston on the same day as Hugo and I also had some meetings there. He suggested that we all go by train (ironically considering the subject of our conversation) which would give us all a good long time (four hours) to meet and to talk. And talk we did. Dan asked lots of questions and made copious notes. He agreed to come back to me. A few days later, he called me. He liked the business and thought we did have an opportunity with our unique publishing platform. Better still, his long-time friend and associate Bob Frankston (another tech über-guru) had used the site and shaved a considerable sum off the price of sending his daughter by air to Australia.

So Dan joined our US board and instantly we were able to plug into the Massachusetts technology world. Not only did Dan introduce us to people relevant to our business but he also provided a fund of ideas including blogging which led to the launch of CheapflightsNews.

3. Stick to what you know best

We did not try to diversify in the USA. Going outside your native market is very hard. To try to do it with a different product is compounding that problem. So the Cheapflights consumer proposition was (and is) very similar to the one that we had been developing successfully for years in the UK.

We did not run any fancy market research. We did not trawl the streets of Manhattan asking passers-by whether or not they would use a website on which you could compare and contrast flight deals (but on which you could not actually buy a flight – that would have to be sourced from one of our travel advertisers). As a market-driving company, and one with a good understanding of what internet users want, we had the courage of our convictions.

4. Adapt quickly to the local market

It is claimed that Oscar Wilde said that the USA and the UK are *'two nations divided by a common language'*. I learned this soon after I arrived in the USA as a student when, during a dinner conversation, I explained that in British general elections it is always important to 'knock up' voters. I realized that in future I would have tread rather more carefully. And I was in turn somewhat surprised when my hostess said how much she liked my pants. Americans say 'mad', we say 'angry'. Closets, trunks and faucets replace cupboards, boots and taps. Purses and suspenders merely cause confusion.

Similarly, American travel terminology is different. While we launched a similar site to that of the UK, we quickly adapted it for the US market. Americans do not have 'return flights', they have 'round trips'. Car hire becomes car rental. Holidays are vacations. And we had to change the navigation system of the website which worked well for the UK but was unsuited to the much more complex USA which has more than 10 times as many departure airports (over 800 at the time of writing).

5. Start cheap

GEC/Marconi and Marks & Spencer may have had their shareholder millions to gamble on American adventures. Alas, we were operating out of cash flow. So an expensive launch, however desirable, was not an option. We were repeatedly told that we needed tens of millions of dollars to launch successfully in the USA (presumably that was for the big TV campaigns that non-market-driving companies have to pay for in order to try to convince consumers that they are in some way different from all the other competitors in their industry). We had not spent very much money in the UK, starting in a serviced office, keeping headcount low, spending negligible amounts on marketing and keeping professional fees to a minimum. We decided to replicate all of that in the USA.

We established our first North American office in Boston. Appropriately called 'Pilot House', it was in an old customs house overlooking Boston harbour (as well as Logan Airport): nothing fancy, one small office, some desks in an open-plan area and otherwise shared facilities (photocopier, meeting room). We started not with an enormous team but just three people. We agonized over every dollar spent. In other words, had we failed we would not have brought the company down. At no stage were we willing to risk the family silver on our international expansion.

The lesson for entrepreneurs is this: taking a business overseas is fraught with risk and is much more complex than anyone might imagine. So mitigate that risk by not betting your company on it. If you fail, write it off as a bad experience but do not write off your company in the process.

6. Hire the right people

Cheapflights USA was set up by Hugo Burge. As my business partner, vice chairman of the company, a major shareholder and product guru, it made sense to have him in charge. Not only did he know every aspect of the Cheapflights business but he also had a very keen understanding of the international flights market. I had studied for one of my Masters' degrees in the USA and had spent much of my own career working for American companies. It was my view that Hugo had the diplomatic and people skills necessary to thrive in what many British people fail to understand is a foreign environment, certainly one which is as different from the UK as any Western European country (in some ways more so). To support him, he took with him one of our most experienced UK travel executives, and then quickly recruited locally an extremely able technology person who also possessed great entrepreneurial drive and instincts. This was the three-strong team that started the American operation.

By 2006 the first wave of our expansion effort had succeeded. Cheapflights reached the top 20 of over 500 travel websites.[1] To cope with our rapid growth, we occupied new corporate offices in Boston's historic School Street (a large floor above the Borders Bookstore). And to oversee the American operation we appointed a general manager who had significant local experience, having worked in a variety of senior roles for one of Massachusetts' leading website companies, Monster.com.

An important point is this. One of the dangers of opening overseas offices is that you create an 'us and them mentality' which can be very destructive if the 'head office' is perceived to be remote and all-powerful. At Cheapflights we tried to mitigate this by encouraging staff to spend time in the different offices. Today Global Marketing is based in Boston, as is the CEO, while leading team members (for example, senior finance and designers) are seconded there from London. This has the merit not only of building on Cheapflights' long UK experience but also ensuring that the company's culture is shared across different offices.

7. Don't give up

Several of our investors were set against an American expansion. And, as we have seen, our first PR company urged us to call it a day. Some of the more established airlines took a bit of convincing to sign up. Hiring good sales people proved harder than we imagined. But as we were not investing a vast amount of money, we could afford to take our time while we overcame the various hurdles.

8. Get yourself a great lawyer

The USA is unbelievably litigious: large American firms will litigate with the slightest excuse. Unlike the UK where you bring in litigation lawyers as a last resort, in the USA, they are often used as an opening salvo, which can be quite alarming. It therefore makes sense early on to arm yourself with a good law firm. We appointed a first-rank American law firm to represent us. This appointment proved invaluable when very early on we were unjustly accused of publishing fares without permission (in fact we not only had permission but were being paid to display those fares). And make sure you get full insurance for any corporate liability.

9. Choose the right location

I agonized about the best office location for a long time. I got down to a short list of four: Silicon Valley, New York, Washington DC (AOL, then a digital behemoth that had reached a market value of $240bn at one stage was located in northern Virginia) and Boston. I ruled out Washington DC and New York on the basis that neither was close to a tech epicentre and that in attracting talent it would be vital to be near other tech companies. In New York rent was astronomically high and we would have the same problem as London: competing against the banks for technology talent. One of these institutions was much later, cruelly described as one of those *'great vampire squids wrapped around the face of humanity relentlessly jamming its blood funnel into anything that smells like money'*. Whatever your view of the usefulness of bankers, however, they are extremely good at 'jamming their blood funnels' into anything that smells like talent, and we could never compete with their huge salary levels and bonuses.

Silicon Valley superficially had attractions: a great climate, technology in abundance, and a track record of successful internet start-ups. But it did have two overwhelming problems which were its time zone, eight hours behind London, and its flying time from London (11 hours). Also, from a British perspective, the culture is that bit further removed. It is not just the dress code; it is all the hype that goes with it, which is so different from British understatement.

So, in the end, I settled on Boston, a decision endorsed by Hugo. It too has access to talent (some of the finest universities in the world, including Harvard and MIT). It is a little more 'understated' and soft-spoken than California, which gels more easily with the Cheapflights culture. It has plentiful high-quality office space (rents are a fraction of London's, even with a strong dollar). And it is only seven hours' flying time from London, with the city centre very close to Logan Airport. On a good day, I could be in the office within half an hour of landing.

10. Control the purse strings

It was of course vital to ensure that good financial controls were in force. The American business was immediately put under the scrutiny of our finance director with the same tight controls as we had put in place in London. I had read too many examples of British companies where 'black holes' had appeared in their foreign operations, and I wanted full visibility. And as if to feed my paranoia, as I was contemplating our launch, one of America's biggest corporations – audited by one of the world's top accountancy firms – went bankrupt. Quite simply it had fabricated its financial condition with an institutionalized, systematic, and creatively-planned accounting fraud. And the now-defunct Enron Corporation had been run, sadly, by someone with whom I had been at business school.

Europe is not America

For entrepreneurs considering overseas expansion, there is no right roadmap which suits every business. Some companies will expand in Europe because there already is an established competitor in the USA despite the vast size of the US domestic market.

Cheapflights has been pondering the issue of European expansion for years. We decided to go to the USA first, and Canada second, but it was only a matter of time before we entered Continental Europe with suitably-constructed foreign-language websites.

By 2009 over half of the European population (some 418 million people if you include Russia and Turkey – larger than the entire population of the USA) were online. This was a trebling of users in just 10 years. Some countries were approaching saturation: in the Netherlands 86% were online, with the UK at 76%.[2]

Many companies have adopted an acquisition strategy to get into the local European markets. At Cheapflights, we decided that the optimal way forward, both in terms of cost and business risk, was to use our own publishing platform and roll it out country by country.

In the first wave of our European expansion, we decided not to open local offices but rather to hire suitably-qualified country nationals and locate them in our London office. Being a melting pot of nationalities, London is not short of European talent.

Many American businesses make the mistake of thinking that Europe is like the USA. The 'European Union' may be a bit deceptive as there remains quite a lot of hostility in the member states towards the concept. Despite the introduction of a single currency by some European Union countries (but not all – for example, not the UK, Poland, Sweden or Denmark), the fact is that Europe remains a continent divided by language, history, religion, culture, laws, customs and food. In the USA, a web developer may relocate quite easily from, say, Boston to San Diego or from Miami to Seattle. Despite the fact that there is now free movement of labour within the EU, the chances of a web developer moving as easily and willingly from Edinburgh to Rome or Barcelona to Stockholm are much less.

If any American business doubts the strength of feeling among Europeans to preserve fiercely their identities they need only to look at: the strong independence movement in Scotland (which has been part of the UK for 300 years); the popularity of the Lega Nord in northern Italy; the antagonism between Walloons and

Flemings in Belgium; the home-grown terrorists of recent years in Northern Ireland and the Basque region; and the horrific events in the former Yugoslavia.

If you want to set up a business in any part of America, the opportunity to roll out that business across the country is very much easier than adding even *one* other European country, let alone all of them.

You might imagine that a virtual digital business might be simpler. But the lessons of the last 15 years tell us the opposite is true. Google is considered to be the most successful American digital business to operate in Europe. It is true that in many European countries it has become the dominant force in search with some staggering market shares: in 2009 it had shares of over 80% in each of the UK, France, Germany and Italy. One source even suggested a 95% share in the Netherlands.[3]

But the problem that Google now faces is only just beginning. First, unlike the USA, where politicians on the whole rather like to support businesses, in Europe they cannot resist meddling, especially in media. Second, the digital expansion has taken the slow-moving politicians and bureaucrats completely by surprise; so much of the relevant legislation is focused more, for example, on the ownership of the TV spectrum and control of newspapers than on new media.

As recently as 2005, with the rise of the internet into its second decade, one individual said that '*after all the excitement of the late 1990s, I suspect many of you in this room did the same, quietly hoping that this thing called the digital revolution would just limp along...Well it hasn't...it won't...and it's a fast developing reality.*[4]

That individual was not a politician or a bureaucrat but someone who, it is said, has printing ink for blood, namely Rupert Murdoch. So if Murdoch was taken by surprise by the digital revolution, what about those who legislate?

The hostility which Google is experiencing among European legislators in Italy, France and Germany demonstrates just how problematic Europe is for creating international digital businesses. The huge differences between the European countries demonstrate one reason why Europe has not yet produced a global internet company on the business scale of an eBay or Google or with a user reach like Facebook or Twitter.

Nevertheless there are a multitude of European internet success stories, and many factors suggest that this is just the beginning. There are many encouraging signs as Saul Klein, one of Europe's leading digital investors, showed in a keynote 2007 presentation. Having reminded his audience that European countries have created global fashion, entertainment and retailing brands, he argued that conditions are better now for the creation of similar internet success.[5]

Europe has never lacked creative or technological talent. But as Klein pointed out, one entirely new phenomenon is the availability of investment capital for digital businesses either from venture capital companies (American firms such as Accel as well as regional firms like Germany's Wellington, the UK's DFJ Esprit or Scandinavia's North Zone Ventures) or from seasoned digital investors such as Klein himself and his father Robin, Oliver Yung, Niklas Zennström and Janus Friis, the Samwer Brothers, Brent Hoberman and Michael Birch.

Howzat Media, a digital investment fund started by Hugo Burge and me, is an example, having invested in several early-stage internet media companies in Europe as well as the USA. As Klein emphasizes, at the start of the century, this European investment ecosystem simply did not exist. It is still small – tiny compared with Silicon Valley – but it is a start.

There is also now a demonstrated track record of companies that have successfully exited such as uSwitch, Kelkoo, LastMinute and LastFM (all to American companies).

Certainly, Europe has proved an attractive hunting ground for American internet companies seeking to fast-track their entry. Simon Murdoch spotted this opportunity way back in 1996 when he founded Book Pages which he then sold in 1998 to Amazon. Likewise in Germany three brothers – Oliver, Alexander and Mark Samwer – have spent more than 10 years closely looking at the American internet scene and imitating the best ideas. Oliver Samwer actually wrote a thesis 'America's Most Successful Startups. Lessons for Entrepreneurs' back in 1998. Particularly liking eBay, he and his brothers quickly put the lessons of that book into practice. They started up an online auction website in Germany called Alando.de.

Within 100 days of launch, the Samwers flipped Alando to eBay for $50m and they were off to the races.[6] The Samwer brothers later founded Jamba, a company that produces ring tones for mobile phones, and then sold it to VeriSign for more than $270m in 2004. More recently (2007), they invested in the German social networking site StudiVZ, only to sell their shares a few months later to the German media conglomerate Holtzbrinck and use the proceeds to invest in Facebook.[7]

Today the Samwers' 'European Founders Fund' continues to invest. Their portfolio includes Nasza-Klasa which is a popular social network in Poland, and Sport1.de, Germany's leading sports portal and operator of the sports community sportsfreunde.de.

France too has seen its share of internet successes, excelling perhaps not surprisingly, at fashion, dating and film. Not surprisingly one of the most notable web companies is the fashion retailer vente-privee. Founded in 2001, vente-privee.com hosts exclusive sales for its 8 million members. It features deeply discounted items from some 850 major brands covering: fashion, fashion accessories, homeware, sports products and electronics. Vente-privee has moved into Germany, Spain, Italy and the UK. Sales in 2009 were over £500m. Recently, they were rumoured to be in exit talks with Amazon at a price tag of $3bn.[8]

The French too have been very successful with their dating site meetic.fr, also founded in 2001 — so successful indeed, that it acquired the European arm of Dallas-based match.com (the dating subsidiary of Barry Diller's internet conglomerate Inter Active Corporation). Match retains a 27% stake in the merged businesses. This is an unusual example of an American internet company selling out to a European one. Meetic, which is a public company, had a market value of over €500m in early 2010. This challenges the misplaced but frequent assumption that American internet companies will automatically dominate the world.

And just as Meetic was not shy about competing with Match, so another French internet company is taking on an American giant: Daily Motion is France's answer to YouTube. Backed with around $60m of funding, Daily Motion claimed recently to be in profit and to have 60 million unique users per month.[9]

Another European success story is far less obvious than most and involves the very un-tech subject of paper dolls. Based in Sweden, it was founded by 'Liisa' (she seems to have but one name, rather like Pele, Madonna or Popeye). According to the company's publicity, Liisa is, apparently, a retired factory worker who, in her late 50s, decided to start this business. In a tale which puts Pierre Omidyar's Pez dispensers in the shade, Liisa, we are told, had a passion since childhood for paper dolls. She used to draw the dolls and the different garments for their wardrobes. More importantly perhaps (and remarkably), she also taught herself web design.

Soon, her personal home page became popular with Swedish teens and in 2004 she upgraded her site and named it Paperdoll Heaven. Just as another famous Swedish export ABBA replaced its precursor names of The Hep Stars and The Hootenanny Singers, so Paperdoll Heaven was renamed and relaunched as Stardoll in 2006. The website has become a fully-fledged online community for young girls. Now backed by Index Ventures and Sequoia Capital, in 2009 it acquired Piczo, the San Francisco-based social network which had been faltering against MySpace and Bebo. The newly-combined network said it would reach more than 20 million teens a month.[10]

So, while Europe has not yet produced its first $10bn internet company, there is no lack of drive or entrepreneurial ambition.

Meanwhile the American internet companies continue their relentless drive into Europe. There is no one strategy that has proved overwhelmingly effective. The travel industry, one of the first to capitalize on the internet and, in so doing, create global players, shows some of the different approaches which can be taken. It is instructive for entrepreneurs to look carefully at these different approaches which again illustrate that as far as international expansion is concerned there is no one 'right answer'.

Expedia (and its subsidiary TripAdvisor) has launched in a variety of countries. In 2008, it acquired Rome-based Venere, a website focused on hotel reservations. The online journal, TheDeal.com, reported a price of between €300m and €350m ($464m and $541m), noting that Venere had grown organically and through acquisition to become one of the largest independent digital players in Europe.[11]

Expedia's competitor Travelocity, having tried starting up in the UK and then finding it painfully slow-going, acquired the British internet company LastMinute.com for £577m in 2005. LastMinute, which had floated just weeks before the market collapsed in 2000, had been on a buying frenzy across Europe. It spent around £260m over four years buying 14 online travel companies in Britain, Germany, France and southern Europe. These included the French Travelprice.com and degriftour.com. At a stroke, Travelocity had established a major bridgehead across Europe as well as acquiring a major UK brand.[12]

But neither Expedia nor Travelocity has transformed itself as a result of its European efforts. For Expedia, during the first nine months of 2009, only 33% of worldwide gross bookings and 35% of worldwide revenue derived from the *whole* of the rest of the world outside the USA.[13]

That is not the case with another major American online travel company, Priceline, whose two successful European acquisitions have pitched the company once again into the major league and have made it one of the most successful global internet companies of the past decade.

Priceline Inc. acquired UK-based Active Hotels for $161m in 2004 and Netherlands-based Bookings seven months later for $133m. Both were leading players in the fast-growing internet hotel reservation services sector. By 2009 Priceline was able to state that Europe represents '*the significant majority*' of its international activities which in turn represented around two thirds of its gross bookings and its consolidated operating income.

Priceline commented: '*We expect that our international operations will represent a growing percentage of our total gross bookings and operating income…over the long term. Because of what we believe to be superior growth rate opportunities associated with international online travel, we intend to continue to invest resources to increase the share of our revenues represented by international consumers and capitalize on international travel demand.'* Of Priceline's 1,780 full-time employees, 1,350 were based in its international offices.[14]

Priceline is perhaps one of the most amazing internet success stories of all. Founded in 1998 by Jay Walker, it went public in 1999. Its share price peaked at $162 valuing Priceline at $11.8bn. Walker's own shares were valued at $5.2bn with the American press hailing him as one of the internet's biggest stars. But the company ran into difficulties and losses spiralled just as the stock market went into free-fall in 2000. The share price collapsed. Walker sold his shares and left the board. Soon afterwards, a new management team led by Jeffery Boyd was installed and realized the strategic opportunity of expanding into the highly-fragmented international hotel bookings arena.[15]

The ability of Boyd to build this international company has yielded stunning results for his shareholders. Priceline.com, perennially considered an also-ran compared with the mighty Expedia, overtook it in November 2009 by market capitalization, with a value of $9.17bn (versus Expedia's $7.21bn).[16]

Japan

Japan has 96 million internet users (5.5% of the world's total).[17]

That great internet survivor Yahoo is often criticized for its lack of focus, especially compared with its rival Google. But the company got at least one thing right and that was its strategy in

Japan. As TechCrunch has put it, Yahoo Japan is *'almost synonymous with the web itself'*. Yahoo Japan was established in 1996 very soon after Yahoo itself was founded. Sensibly, it decided not to control its Japanese venture but to partner with the giant Japanese conglomerate SoftBank. SoftBank's founder Masayoshi Son (who has a degree from UC Berkeley and is now one of Japan's richest men) doubles as Yahoo Japan's chairman.

Yahoo's Japanese website bears little resemblance to the Yahoo of the West, and the scale of its business stretches far beyond its Western counterpart. It has diversified (in a typically Japanese way) into a myriad of businesses including telecommunications and media. In the Japanese internet sector it is dominant. Its auction business, for example, has been successful whereas eBay has struggled in Japan. The huge mistake eBay made was that it rebuffed an approach from SoftBank's Son who wanted a majority of eBay Japan. eBay preferred instead, hubristically, to launch its own website in 2000. That failure to partner with SoftBank cost eBay dearly, not just in Japan but in other Asian markets where Yahoo Japan competed. As Meg Whitman admitted *'With twenty twenty hindsight it was probably one of the bigger strategic mistakes we've made.'*[18]

Even the mighty Google, which has chosen not to have a local partner, is finding it tough in Japan as it tries to compete there with Yahoo's search business. Google's share of the market is only 40% (rather modest for Google) versus Yahoo's of around 50%.[19] However in 2010 Yahoo Japan announced that it had chosen Google to power its web searches and, under the terms of the deal, split the revenues. This was the potential leap forward for Google to obtain search leadership in this important market.

Amazon, however, shows that it is possible to go it alone. Bezos, who has always put international expansion at the heart of Amazon's strategy (barely half of Amazon's sales are now in the domestic USA),[20] launched in Japan in 2000. According to one Japanese research company, Amazon maintains rapid sales growth in Japan, increasing them by 18.2% to ¥260bn ($2.9bn) in fiscal 2008, a year that witnessed decreases for most supermarkets and department stores. About the undisclosed profitability of Amazon Japan, the research company opined, *'The figure is thought to be far beyond those of other retail companies.'*[21]

The key point here is whether or not you need a local partner to crack Japan. The experience of Yahoo and Google suggests that you do; Amazon leads to the opposite conclusion. My experience suggests that, to succeed in Japan, where both culture and language are so different from those of the West, it makes sense to find a powerful local partner.

China

China is even more difficult than Japan. Entrepreneurs need to be aware of two contradictory factors about this market: it has a free-wheeling approach to business, but, at the same time, it also has a very strong centralized government that is anything but freewheeling. That government also takes a particularly keen interest in the internet.

One in five users of the internet worldwide, 360 million, are now in China, 50% more than the USA which trails in second place with 228 million (13% of world users).[22] But the Chinese internet opportunity, while vast, has eluded most Western companies.

Yahoo was one of the first foreign internet companies to open its doors there in 1999. Six years later, after struggling to make headway, it sold out to a Chinese company, Alibaba, China's largest business-to-business e-commerce website. Yahoo owns 39% of Alibaba. Yahoo has steadily lost share in China's internet search market since that deal (now around 6% versus 21% when it sold out), although its stake in the broadly-based Alibaba has been overall financially lucrative, recently estimated at $3bn.

The performance of Yahoo's brand in China is not critical for Alibaba or for Yahoo, which doesn't any longer earn revenue directly from China Yahoo. Carol Bartz, Yahoo's CEO, said in 2009 '*Yahoo has no reason to sell its stake in Alibaba, or to run its own brand in China. I think we actually have a bigger play just riding the fortune of Alibaba than we ever could have done being Yahoo in China.*'[23]

But there is a non-financial element to Yahoo's shareholding and that is the PR aspect of its Chinese activities. In 2006, it was disclosed that Yahoo China had given the Chinese police information that helped jail a dissident who had used Yahoo e-mail. One US Congressman castigated Yahoo executives calling them moral 'pygmies' for cooperating with Beijing. This is not the sort of publicity that any company enjoys, let alone one that has to compete fiercely for user loyalty around the world.

But if Yahoo has found China a problem that is nothing compared with Google whose spats with the Chinese government have been headline news and whose tribulations have involved both President Obama and Secretary of State Hilary Clinton.

In 2006 Google entered China with high hopes; but it censored some of its results bringing on it the wrath of human rights activists. Tensions with the Chinese government mounted and in January 2010 the company said it was considering exiting China, alleging that it had been cyber-attacked by the government in an attempt to access the Gmail accounts of Chinese human rights campaigners.

But behind the headline-grabbing politics, there lies the business history of Google in China. It is natural that the world's largest and most successful media company would want to enter China, the biggest internet market of all. But just as Meg Whitman had thought eBay could go it alone in Japan, so Google believed that because the rest of the world had adopted its search methodology so quickly, the Chinese would do the same.

Rarely for the Google management team, they were proved quite wrong. By 2009 it was still lagging way behind the market leader Baidu. One report suggested Baidu accounted for 74.1% of the total search request volume in the first quarter of 2009, compared with Google's share of 20.9%, although Google took nearly one third of China's search revenues.[24]

Baidu's success against Google is instructive. It is true that it was well established when Google entered the Chinese market (though we have seen how Google destroyed Alta Vista in the USA). But in the USA Google launched with a better product than Alta Vista's. In China, users preferred Baidu's search box which was much better suited to Chinese characters. Baidu was shrewder at attracting traffic. For instance, it offered a wildly popular music download service – Google offered its equivalent only in 2009.[25]

eBay too has found China a step too far. It all started well. In 2002, it bought a 33% stake in EachNet, then the leading Chinese auction house, and in 2003 it purchased the remaining shares for $150m. Briefly, it controlled 80% of the Chinese e-commerce market. Then it was completely outmanoeuvred by Jack Ma, a former lecturer in English, who, in 1999, had founded Alibaba.com (the company that acquired Yahoo's Chinese business). In 2003, the year that eBay bought out EachNet, Ma set up Taobao.com.

eBay charged for listings, while Taobao did not. eBay also did not offer ways for buyers and sellers to chat online. It feared they would lose transaction fees as users would transact off the site. Taobao understood that live conversations were necessary for Chinese consumers to cultivate trust, and offered an instant-message service to allow them to haggle over deals. According to one source, eBay also put its Chinese auctions on web servers outside the country, resulting in a sluggish service that was difficult for some Chinese citizens to access. By 2006 eBay had had enough and folded its Chinese operations into a joint venture in which the majority was held by local company Tom Online. Taobao has become the largest retail platform in China.[26]

China illustrates the huge difficulty that internet businesses face in expanding abroad. But as the internet globalizes, the opportunities for cross-border expansion will simply grow and grow.

Jack Ma said that *'eBay believed they were smarter than Chinese local people.'* So my advice to any entrepreneur thinking of expanding overseas is find yourself local people as quickly as possible and listen very, very carefully to what they have to say. Do your homework and never underestimate the problems. However hard competing in your own country is, moving overseas will be even harder. However, one UK company, which almost went under in its domestic market, found its salvation in overseas operations. Auction site QXL, founded by an FT journalist in 1997, successfully floated in 1999 and then merged with a German rival called Ricardo in 2000. Later that year, following the collapse of the stock market, its shares lost 99% of their value. But QXL continued to pursue a cunning international strategy: focus its auction websites in countries where eBay was still weak, most notably throughout Scandinavia and Eastern Europe. It did this so successfully that when it was taken over in late 2007 it was for £1bn.[27]

So there are a number of key lessons here for entrepreneurs:

- You can mitigate risk by integrating as quickly as possible with the local market, especially by doing your homework thoroughly, networking and hiring locally, by sticking to your core competence, by adapting quickly, by limiting investment, by hiring the right people and integrating them with the company at large, by persevering, choosing the right location and ensuring excellent financial controls.
- Each new market needs its own consideration: in the USA, for example, hiring a good law firm is essential.
- Europe is an extremely complex series of markets. It is not one country. But increasingly it is producing successful internet

businesses. The travel industry, already relatively mature by internet standards, shows the different ways of expanding across Europe by start-ups, by acquisition or a combination of the two.

- Both Japan and China are very tough markets for foreign companies to crack and, in each case, a local partner might be advisable.

- Sometimes opportunities can be discovered in the most unexpected territories as QXL, a minnow compared to its mighty US competitor eBay, discovered in Scandinavia and Eastern Europe.

Chapter Eight

THE FUTURE

Embrace the inevitable and exploit its occurrence.
(attributed to Charles de Gaulle)

The pace of change

The X Factor has been one of the great TV successes of recent times regularly pulling in an audience of some 15 million viewers, roughly a quarter of the UK's population. For four years running, the show produced Britain's best-selling Christmas single record, an enormous achievement in a country in which the Christmas Number One has achieved huge cultural status, with previous winners including the Beatles, Queen and Pink Floyd.

But December 2009 saw something very strange happening. *The X Factor*'s winner, an 18-year-old called Joe McElderry, failed to make it to the top. After four years of supremacy, *The X Factor* had stumbled. How could this TV juggernaut have been stopped in its tracks? It happened because of the internet; more specifically, because of Facebook. An Essex couple, Jon and Tracy Morter, had organized a campaign on the social networking site which pro-pelled another music act, Rage Against the Machine (not a very Christmassy name perhaps), to the coveted Number One slot.

Here was the power of new media laid bare: the might of ITV's most successful show bested by a skilful Facebook campaign that cost the Morters precisely nothing. And Facebook proved more potent. Simon Cowell, the media svengali behind *The X Factor*, was so impressed by the Morters' efforts that he immediately offered them both jobs: '*It could be in marketing or even running the company!*'[1]

Just a few weeks later, on the other side of the Atlantic, something extraordinary happened too. The Pepsi Cola Corporation announced that, for the first time in 23 years, it would *not* be showing TV ads during the Super Bowl, consistently one of the most-watched television programmes of the year. Pepsi had spent some $142m over the years on its Super Bowl ads but now it announced that, instead of this TV spend, it would allocate $20m to a social media campaign called the 'Pepsi Refresh Project'. Pepsi, which employs some of the most sophisticated marketers in the world, clearly believed that it could derive more benefit from $20m spent on worthy projects via a Facebook poll, with all the buzz generated from this philanthropy, than by a traditional glitzy ad slot.[2]

Ironically, another major corporation *did* decide to run a Super Bowl ad for the very first time – perhaps to demonstrate to the world that it was somehow worried about competition for its market-dominating product following a fall in its US January market share from 65.7 to 65.4%: Google.[3]

The pace of change has accelerated since 2000, the dot.com 'collapse' notwithstanding. The first 10 years of the new century witnessed, among others, the launch of Google's AdWords and the company's IPO, Wikipedia (which went live in 2001 and was being used by a third of adult American internet users within seven years of starting up),[4] YouTube, Facebook and Twitter.

So what will the next 10 years bring?

Connecting the world

Half-way through the second decade of its life, the internet was proving more than merely disruptive. It was causing seismic changes in the way people were doing business. We have seen how advertising has been transformed in just a few years. As I mentioned in Chapter Six, the increased measurability of internet advertising has solved John Wanamaker's conundrum. Wanamaker was the department store king who had famously remarked that half of the money he spent on advertising was wasted, the trouble being he did not know which half. With digital advertising, you know exactly how well your advertising performs – all of it not just half. You can build up much more intimate relationships with customers. And you can improve your targeting to an extent unknown in the old economy. Brand owners see the opportunity to have one-to-one contact with consumers that was previously impossible.

But there are still some in advertising agencies that are terrified by change. They are slowing down the shift to digital because they believe it will erode their margins. They still encourage their clients to spend and spend on expensive and unproductive media. But advertising agencies that fail to embrace digital more fully will lose their clients, who are desperate to have the intimate, interactive and targeted relationship with their customers that digital media provides.

Some recent statistics from Google make the point about the sheer pace of change: there are now 42 million online shoppers in the UK (71% growth over the last two years); 17p in every consumer pound is being spent online (almost twice the level of the USA); and nearly £70bn of UK business is done on the internet (compared with only £87m in 2000).[5]

When Borders Bookstores closed all of its 45 shops in the UK in late 2009, it was just another sign of the changes being wrought by digital technology. One UK retail consultancy estimates that, by 2013, books purchased online will rise from 19% of the market to 30%. Play.com, a major UK e-tailer, reported that its book sales rose 55% in the first three quarters of 2009. All this is happening when e-books are just starting to be sold in the UK. Apple's entry into e-books via its new iPad device will accelerate sales of e-readers. Sales of these devices are expected to reach 12 million globally in 2010 (up from 5 million in 2009 and 1 million in 2008).[6] What will happen to bookshops when e-books become *really* popular? My guess is that small specialist bookshops which offer a highly-personalized service and a pleasing ambiance – like Daunts in London – will survive, just like small specialist travel agencies, but that the more generalist chains will follow Borders UK into oblivion.

In marked contrast to Borders UK, 2009 was a sensational year for Amazon whose share price soared by a stratospheric 166%. USA Today's index (calculated by Dow Jones) for the top-quoted internet companies showed that overall their share prices had increased by 66.7% in just one year. Some stocks had done even better than Amazon: travel behemoths Expedia and Priceline went up by 221% and 203% respectively, and Chinese search engine Baidu by 218%.[7]

Infrastructure

Behind the success of new media lies the infrastructure. Because broadband access and the speed of broadband are both invisible, they have perhaps not received the attention they have deserved as key measures of a country's progress. Yet just as roads were a key measure in the twentieth century, so broadband will be one of the key measures of the new century.

Politicians are, as always, far behind the times and have been remarkably slow to understand why broadband is important. It is true that in the five years between 2003 and 2008 there were some important advances. In the UK broadband access increased from just 3 million to 17 million connections (an annual growth rate of 41%), while in the USA it went from 26 million to 76 million connections (a 24% annual increase).

But a recent study showed just how far behind many Western governments are in ensuring that fast broadband reaches every household. The research grouped the world's nations into five categories: ready for tomorrow, comfortably enjoying today's applications, meeting the needs of today's applications, below today's applications threshold and leapfrog opportunity. Not surprisingly the best performers are South Korea, Japan and Sweden.

The USA, that many imagine is cutting-edge, is way down the list, sitting in the second category behind both the Czech Republic and Slovakia. And Britain too has nothing to cheer about with its ranking all the way down in the third category.[8]

There is a simple necessity for high-speed broadband, not only for wealth creation and entrepreneurship but also for reducing the costs of the public sector. In addition, the gap between rich and poor is now exacerbated by the fact that many of the poorest in society and those living in remote rural communities are unable to take advantage of the new economy. Providing access to all is neither simple nor cheap; but a century ago, there were similar arguments about the road network: ultimately universal access will not be an option but a practical necessity.

It is inevitable that the future demand for digital offerings, for example video, will require much more bandwidth. In other words, as applications become more data intensive, the need for faster download speeds is imperative. So, the longer we wait for our governments to react, the bigger the divisions will become between the 'haves' and the 'have nots', between the urban communities located near telephone exchanges and the rural communities deemed too expensive to connect – and eventually between the countries that understand the way communication is moving and those whose leaders seem rooted in a different century.

Many of my own activities have centred on websites that use the power of digital technology to help consumers find the best deals. It seems a shame that those who need this access most are being denied it because the infrastructure remains below par. There are no more deserving groups in society to have high-speed broadband than the old, the infirm and the less affluent. These are people for whom digital access can be particularly life-enhancing, offering a means to work, socialize, shop, access public services and save money.

A recent piece of research produced by PricewaterhouseCoopers (PwC) found that the average UK family would miss out on savings totalling up to £560 a year if they did not use the internet to shop around for the cheapest deals on products like energy, insurance and household items.

Martha Lane Fox, the co-founder of LastMinute.com and the British government's Digital Czar, told the BBC Radio 4's *Today* programme:

> *As a consumer, you are missing out on great savings if you don't shop online, let alone the fact that more and more government services are going to become digitised...*

> *It is worth fighting for the rights of people to have the same choices and access to the same benefits as all of us who are web-enabled.*

To an extent Lane Fox is right. The problem is, however, not so much about fighting for rights as about government creating the conditions for universal access. This is not alas something the private sector can accomplish entirely alone, any more than the private sector unaided can build a country's transport infrastructure. That is the lesson of South Korea and Japan where government participation has encouraged the phone companies to provide the access.

But as the UK dithers, other Western governments have understood the urgency. Tiny Estonia moved rapidly to embrace the digital revolution and has one of the most advanced electronic infrastructures in the world with a government that is fully digitized.

Finland, with some 5 million inhabitants, was once a country chiefly famous for the composer Sibelius and a language that no one outside Finland could speak. Today it is known (at least in technology circles) as the country that produced Linus Torvalds, the software engineer who created the kernel of the Linux operating system, and Nokia, the world's largest manufacturer of mobile phones (40% of the global market in 2009).

Now, Finland has become the first country to declare fast broadband internet access to be a legal right. The telecom companies in Finland will be required to provide all Finnish citizens with a high-speed 1 Mbps broadband internet connection.

According to Laura Vilkkonen, the legislative counsellor for the Ministry of Transport and Communications, the plan is to provide all Finns with even faster broadband speeds (100 Mbps) by 2015. *'We think it's something you cannot live without in modern society. Like banking services or water or electricity, you need internet connection.'*[9]

Privacy

Back in the mid-1990s I worked in the Prime Minister's Policy Unit in Number 10 Downing Street. One of my responsibilities as a special adviser to John Major was a consideration of the merits of reintroducing the identity card. The last time that the UK introduced such a card was during World War II, and my own view was (and is) that this type of card has no place in a modern democracy and is quite alien to British culture. Such a card was merely another step on the road to a Big Brother society where the government would be in a position to snoop on and monitor the activities of its citizens. Happily, John Major and his cabinet quickly dismissed the idea, only for it later to be embraced with some gusto by Tony Blair and the incoming Socialist administration after they came to power in 1997. The new coalition government has now scrapped it.

Needless to say, the advocates of the identity card trot out familiar arguments: the 'war against terror'; controlling illegal immigration; and halting benefit fraud. All this sounds logical and perhaps persuasive. But the fact is that the British version of the identity card, containing so much personal data, is an effective licence for the government to spy on its citizens and allow others too to do so (assuming that the government would be unable to keep such records confidential – at least a possibility given recent leaks: remember it tried its very hardest to keep those MP expense claims under wraps). This is the 'dark scenario' which causes so much opposition to the card.

Similarly, and as always with new technology, there is a dark side to the internet. Indeed there are *many* dark sides. But one of the very darkest relates to the protection of privacy. '*If you have something that you don't want anyone to know, maybe you shouldn't be doing it in the first place*', said Eric Schmidt recently in what was considered by many to be an unusually incendiary remark that caused howls of protest from civil liberties campaigners.[10]

Curiously, it was not Google's privacy policies, its use of cookies or even the storing of vast amounts of data which brought it into controversy in the UK. Rather, it was its '*Street View*' function which allows Google users to have a bird's-eye photographic view of virtually every street. Angry residents of the Buckinghamshire village of Broughton blocked the driver of a Google *Street View* car when he started taking photographs of their homes. Police were called after villagers staged a protest accusing Google of invading their privacy and 'facilitating crime'. As one of those interviewed explained, 'an Englishman's home is his castle', not perhaps something which is fully understood in Google's Californian HQ.[11]

When asked about his company's policy, a Google spokesman said that you could quite easily opt out of *Street View* if you did not wish for your house to appear. Just like his boss Eric Schmidt, this seems to show a woeful misunderstanding of people's growing concerns. 'Opting out' is not really an answer.

In Germany it was the government that found *Street View* a problem. It caused the ire of the consumer affairs minister (*'private things are dragged to the global public'*, he said) and the Chancellor herself had to intervene to give Google the go-ahead.[12]

But even if Google continuously works on improving its privacy policies – which it does – it will be the very nature of the company's scale and strength that ensures that it remains a focus of concern.

Google is not alone: Facebook has also rarely been out of the spotlight. In early 2009 the social networking site caused its own uproar. It asked its users to update their privacy settings as part of a renewal to its terms of service. There was a storm of complaints from its users who feared that the new terms gave Facebook the right – in perpetuity – to use their photos, messages and other content for marketing or to sell to advertisers.[13]

Critics said that the changes were unwelcome and that the new settings were leading users to reveal more information than they wanted to. This was not Facebook's first brush with privacy issues but it was its biggest storm to date, and it quickly backtracked on some of the changes.[14]

Concerns about online privacy are very frequently voiced and it is a legitimate concern. But there is a curious paradox here: at the very same time as concerns about the online invasion of privacy appear to be growing, there is a massive 'counter-current' that is moving in precisely the opposite direction – namely, the extraordinary inclination of many millions of internet users to make online disclosures about their private lives that are not simply personal (the vacuous tweets of 'C list' celebrities), but also, in many cases, sensitive, confidential or downright intimate. In fact it seems there is literally nothing that is too embarrassing for internet users to broadcast to the world about themselves.

The paradox is demonstrated too by the social networking websites. On the one hand, they will almost always have privacy policies whose terms tend to be carefully drafted by lawyers in order to comply with all applicable data protection legislation. Yet, at the same time, they encourage and facilitate their users to throw privacy to the wind by uploading and broadcasting data that is, very often, extremely private indeed.

The issues surrounding data protection will become even greater and the internet companies themselves will need to be *far* more sensitive in their approach. Individuals will need to show more restraint in what they post online. If the wife of the head of the

UK's intelligence service MI5 could post a photo on Facebook showing her husband in his Speedo swimwear, clearly better education is required, especially for children. When I was growing up, I was warned by my parents not to accept sweets or lifts from strangers. Now those warnings need to embrace posting photos and messages on the internet. Parents and teachers need to be more alert to the dangers and more forceful in preventing children from indiscretions which they will later regret.

In early 2010, a survey – which questioned personnel managers at the top 100 companies in the UK, USA, Germany and France – found that 70% admitted to having rejected a candidate because of his or her online behaviour. Facebook and Twitter checks are now as important in job selection as a CV or an interview.[15]

Everyone loves the positive side of the digital economy: the ease of search, the personalization, the speed of communication, the free flow of information. But if people insist on sharing with the world their most private details, they need to understand fully the consequences.

Traditional media

David Gestetner, a Hungarian entrepreneur who emigrated to London, was the inventor of the Gestetner stencil duplicator, an important piece of office equipment that allowed production of numerous copies of documents quickly and inexpensively. By the 1960s, Gestetner, the eponymous company which he founded and which was still run by his family, was a world leader in the copying industry. It was growing rapidly. And it was hugely profitable.

One day, an executive from an American company which had developed a new line of office products called on Gestetner. He offered the company a European partnership with his employers but Gestetner turned him away. His next call was on a diversified British leisure company called Rank, which saw merit in the partnership and signed up for it. The new product line suggested to Gestetner was plain paper photocopiers; the American company was Xerox; and the new partnership it formed was Rank Xerox.

Xerox and its new European joint venture prospered while Gestetner shrank rapidly, its stencil duplicators being no match for the new-fangled photocopiers. The mistake Gestetner made was to try to protect its core product, not realizing that the new photocopier would put an end to it.

The Gestetner story is a very familiar one – namely, businesses that wither because their products are in due course superseded by a superior invention that is more attractive to consumers. This has happened hundreds of times in the history of commerce, and continues to do so.

Many traditional media companies now provide a classic example. The fact is that increasing numbers of people prefer to receive their content via the internet than by traditional means of transmission which is why newspaper and magazine circulation has slumped in recent years. There is little that traditional media owners can do about this, so they should be embracing change much more quickly instead of bemoaning it – or, worse, trying to curtail it.

Moreover, new media in fact offers enormous opportunities as Michael Kinsley, who founded the online *Slate* magazine back in 1996, demonstrated. A decade later, Arianna Stassinopoulos Huffington founded the online *Huffington Post* and Tina Brown, *The Daily Beast*. Both Kinsley and Brown had extensive experience, as editors, of the traditional printed magazine world, in Kinsley's case *The New Republic* and *Harper's*, in Brown's, *Vanity Fair* and *The New Yorker*.

Because of the low start-up costs, it is much easier to serve a specialized reading audience online. For example, in the travel industry, there have been a number of influential news and blogging websites including e-tid, TravelMole, The Boot, Travolution and Tnooz.

I do not believe for a moment that professional journalism is under threat from the blogosphere, 'citizen journalism' or from the tweets of millions of amateur writers. If you believe that the era of Woodward and Bernstein has died, you have only to look at the 2009 work of *The Daily Telegraph*'s team on the story of MPs expenses. After years of obfuscation, during which MPs tried to prevent exposure of their expenses claims to the general public, it was *The Daily Telegraph* that finally uncovered the secrets, analysed them and fingered the culprits, some of whom went on, as they say in the British vernacular, 'to help the police with their enquiries'.

In 1994, the distinguished journalist and writer Nicholas Coleridge wrote a book called *Paper Tigers: Latest Greatest Newspaper Tycoons and How They Won the World*.[16] Coleridge could hardly have imagined what would happen in the 15 years since that book was published. But while the century-old reign of the media barons may be in its death throes, there are still opportunities for news entrepreneurs and journalists, but in online media rather than print.

The struggle to maintain copyright

The traditional media owners do have a valid argument about copyright abuse. Rupert Murdoch, as we have seen, has been especially hostile towards Google. But it is not just old media that is suffering from online copyright infringement. For instance, the relatively new medium of electronic games (a sector in which the UK has hitherto excelled) is hard hit by the problem. To take just one example from thousands, within 10 days of the official launch of the popular electronic game *Spore*, more than half a million people had downloaded a pirated version of it using peer-to-peer (P2P) technology – around £15m of lost sales.[17]

Music and film too are badly affected: indeed, all of the so-called 'creative content industries' are actually or potentially threatened. This is bad news for poor old UK PLC, as the creative content industries account for more than 6% of our somewhat fragile GDP, and constitute one of the sectors that we can justifiably call world class.

The problem here is that Pandora's Box has been opened. People are now used to free services via the internet. There is a huge difference, however, between a legitimate free service (such as the email service Gmail or the free version of Spotify) and content that has been pirated. For the latter it is reasonable to expect stiffer penalties and more aggressive policing, for cyber theft is no more forgivable than the physical version. Individuals need to take more responsibility, understanding that receiving stolen property via the internet is no different to receiving stolen physical goods.

As for legitimate free services, more pricing models will emerge to ensure that media owners are compensated. Micro-payments for content will become the norm with much faster and easier online payment systems akin to some of the mobile payment approaches. I doubt if people will pay a monthly subscription for *The Times* online, in the way they might for ft.com (especially with the licence-funded BBC obliged to provide free news). But if they see a story they want to read by, say, a favourite columnist, users may be willing to pay a few pence to read it. This was the payment approach which made iTunes a $3bn dollar business within four years of launch.

By early 2010 one entrepreneur realized that there might well be a market in actually *paying* writers, journalists, bloggers, musicians and other creators of digital content. He founded a website called Flattr which involves members paying a fixed monthly fee and then divvying out the proceeds according to which clicks they make (participating websites will display a Flattr button). A little ironic twist: the entrepreneur whose idea this is turns out to be none other than Peter Sunde, whose Swedish Pirate Bay website had been pursued to the courts by film and videomakers alleging infringement of copyright. In 2009 Sunde and three colleagues were found guilty, sentenced to a year in prison and fined €2.7m. They have appealed.[18]

Netopoly

John D. Rockefeller was the founder, chairman and major share-holder of Standard Oil. The company made him a billionaire and eventually the richest man in modern history. Standard Oil, an integrated oil-producing, transporting, refining, and marketing company, became the largest oil refiner in the world and was one of the world's first and largest multinational corporations – until it was broken up by the US Supreme Court in 1911 into 34 independent companies.

For most of the twentieth century, American Telephone and Telegraph (AT&T) – sometimes known as 'Ma Bell' – enjoyed a near-total monopoly on long-distance telephone services in the USA. AT&T also controlled 22 Bell operating companies which provided by far the largest local telephone service to most of the USA. In 1982, AT&T settled a 1974 US Department of Justice antitrust suit. Under the settlement, AT&T agreed to divest its local operations, which were subsequently split into seven independent regional companies known as 'Baby Bells'.

It is a generally-held belief in democratic free market economies that monopolies are a bad thing and regulators take a keen interest in them. Microsoft has been investigated extensively by both the US Justice Department and the European Commission and it seems inevitable that the newest technology giant, Google, will suffer the same fate.

Google has for years provided consumers with wonderful products, all the more appealing because they are free. Google Search,

Google News, Google Maps, and Gmail are just some of the applications used by hundreds of millions of internet users. But the problem Google has is that it needs to diversify to maintain its stunning growth rate. And the more it spreads its tentacles, the more likely it is to fall foul of monopolies legislation.

Already Google has been investigated in the USA, for example, for its acquisition of DoubleClick. Google has come up against the French publishing industry, the German newspaper and magazine industry, and the Italian broadcaster Mediaset (which is owned by the Italian Prime Minster Silvio Berlusconi). In so doing, Google seems to have antagonized the French, German and Italian governments. This reminds me of Lady Bracknell's remark in Oscar Wilde's *The Importance of Being Ernest*: '*To lose one parent, Mr Worthing, may be regarded as a misfortune; to lose both looks like carelessness.*'

In 2010 the Italian assault on Google stepped up a notch. In Milan, a judge sentenced three senior Google executives (including rather bizarrely the former finance director) in absentia to six-month suspended sentences for violation of privacy. Prosecutors claimed Google did not act fast enough to remove from Google video a widely-viewed clip posted in 2006 showing a group of teenage boys harassing an autistic boy.[19]

Early 2009 saw Google tread on some big British toes too. Just a whisper can frighten markets. Google launched a property portal in Australia in August 2009, allowing estate agents to list properties free of charge along with pictures taken from its Street View service and details from Google maps. A logical expansion of Google's activities perhaps. Then just four months later, in

December, there was a rumour in the UK that Google was talking to estate agents with a view to launching its own UK property portal. RightMove PLC, the leading property search company in the UK valued at £600m (as at 4 February 2010) saw its shares marked down by 10% as a result.

In the UK there are some very powerful media groups that have also invested in property portals – including, to date, Rupert Murdoch's NewsCorp and Lord Rothermere's Daily Mail and General Trust, the two biggest UK newspaper groups. If the rumours were true, Google would, in pursuing this new line of business, find itself up against some highly influential opposition.

Just as the French, Germans and Italians are all moving against Google, in the UK criticism reached a crescendo when *The Sunday Times* (owned by NewsCorp) revealed that Google (quite legally) paid virtually no tax on its £1.6bn UK advertising revenue, diverting its advertising income to its Irish subsidiary, and thus avoiding a tax bill of more than £450m. *The Sunday Times* estimated that about 13% of Google's global revenues now come from the UK, and 770 staff are based at its London offices.[20]

Now Google has entered the phone market. Fair enough, you might say. But then opening an online phone store and selling Google-branded Nexus One phones directly to consumers placed Google in direct competition with the mobile phone companies, while simultaneously encouraging them to use Google software and services. Remember the big shoes tale, the story of how the US online retailer of oversized shoes suffered when it lost its rankings on Google's search engines: well, how much do mobile phone stores rely on the search traffic that Google now supplies? Four months later Google closed its web-based store.

No matter how ethically Google is run, no matter how often the company alludes to its 'Don't be evil' philosophy, no matter how great its innovations are, the sheer scale of its activities globally means that it is now under the microscope of legislators and regulators who will most likely be forced by public opinion at some stage to take action to limit its reach.

The global nature of new technology and its speed to market mean that, for the first time in the history of capitalism, it is not simply national and regional monopolies that are an issue for legislators, but also global monopolies and near-monopolies.

So it was just a matter of time before Google's affairs came under scrutiny. Early in 2010 the chief executive of one of the largest British companies, telecoms giant Vodafone, called on regulators to take a close look at Google's dominance of the search market *'before it is too late'*.[21] Within days the call was answered when the European Commission announced a preliminary probe into Google's search advertising activities, the very business which has been the core of Google's success.

An ironic coda to this probe: it was prompted apparently by none other than Microsoft, a company who itself has been punished with the biggest single antitrust fine in EU history.

For entrepreneurs, the issues surrounding Google and its growth are far more than legal niceties. Google is currently the most powerful company on the internet. It is a major provider of services to the internet industry as well as being a worldwide gateway to websites. What happens to it will touch all internet businesses big and small.

Convergence: computers, phones, notebooks and iPads – internet to go, please

Ever since I became actively involved with digital media, one of the most discussed issues has been when exactly there would be convergence between computers and mobile devices. It has been a gradual process. Computers get smaller and smaller (I have written this book on a wafer-thin Sony VAIO) and mobile phones are becoming smarter and smarter. Now the smart-phone is no longer just the device beloved by harassed investment bankers, it has moved into the mainstream.

Consumer choice has suddenly blossomed: the Palm Pre, Motorola's Droid, Blackberries, Nokias and of course the iPhone (and now Google's own effort, the Nexus One). This means lower prices and accelerating functionality. Who, a few years ago, would have predicted that Apple or Google, two of the companies who themselves have propelled the digital revolution, would be selling phones?

The content of such phones has also improved beyond recognition, not just in terms of the thousands of application available (known as 'apps'), but also of the ability for users to access such favourites as Facebook and Twitter while on the move. So much of content used on the internet is well suited to mobile. Maps, naturally. But think about hotel or restaurant reviews: you arrive in a city and you have nowhere to stay and no clue where to eat. Now the smart-phone can sort all that out for you. Just like the personal computer, which started with a limited number of functions (spreadsheets, word processing, emails), suddenly the smart-phone has become a 'must have'.

One story reported in late 2009 seemed to herald the smart-phone's coming-of-age. Drink-driving is one of the banes of the modern age. In the USA there is an average of 36 drink-driving deaths *a day*. Few people realize that in 2001 – remembered for the worst terrorist atrocity in American history – some 17,400 people were killed in the USA as a result of drink-driving.[22]

How do you use digital technology to help prevent these tragedies? In December 2009 the Colorado Department of Transportation launched a free iPhone application to help party-goers calculate their blood alcohol levels. The application, called RU Buzzed, was, according to *The Wall Street Journal*, downloaded more than 40,000 times in its first month. The application (which includes a lengthy disclaimer explaining that individuals do vary in their alcohol tolerance) prompts users to enter their personal details, then calculates and displays a blood alcohol content number. Even if you're under the legal limit of 0.08%, it might say '*You're buzzed!*' and warn you that '*You could be arrested for impaired driving. Designate a sober driver.*'

The fact that such an application could be developed by a state agency to deal with a social problem shows just how important and all-pervasive these devices may be in the years ahead. It is one thing for an investment banker to use a smart-phone to answer emails at the dinner table (a classic, if discourteous, use of smart-phones in their first iteration). It is quite another for, say, teenage children to use one to check they are safe to drive after a night out on the town. And in Colorado's major cities, R U Buzzed has an added feature which uses GPS technology to let the user locate a cab with a tap of the phone.[23]

One simple reason why the smart-phone will continue its inexorable rise is what I would describe as the digital generation, those born in the 1990s, who have known nothing except a society in which computer and mobile phone availability is a given. In the USA there are around 74 million people under the age of 18.[24] In the UK that figure is around 11 million.[25]

This generation carries mobile phones even if they are still too young to have their own computer, and increasingly they will be using smart-phones. This of course is the generation that will provide the new customers for online commerce, familiarized with the technology from an early age, expert at multi-tasking (eating, sending texts, looking at Facebook all at the same time) and who are used to instant gratification.

In 2009, according to the research company IDC, 171 million smart-phones were sold worldwide, with the market growing year-on-year by 39% in the final quarter – an explosion in sales in a year when a deep recession has dampened consumer expenditure overall. For businesses there is a huge opportunity. In 2009, for example, US mobile advertising was only $760m. But according to eMarketer, the business information service, this figure will rise to $3.3bn by 2013.[26] The launch of new devices such as Apple's iPad will merely accelerate the whole take-up of the internet on the move. I envisage a time when everyone will have a single mobile device. Currently I usually travel with a laptop, a smart-phone, an electronic bookreader, a digital camera and an iPod (as well as an electric toothbrush). This is clearly an absurdity, with the plugs, leads and chargers alone a logistical nightmare. Already GPS device manufacturer Tom Tom has introduced a $100 iPhone app which removes the need to buy its hardware, while Google has released a free road-directions service on devices running on its Android mobile phone operating system.[27]

I suspect that in a few years' time I will own a uni-device which will make even today's sexy Amazon Kindle seem like an eight-track cartridge player (if you are under 40, ask your parents or grandparents to tell you what an eight-track cartridge player is). Sadly, I cannot see a time when my uni-device will brush my teeth – but who knows.

The global internet

Peter Drucker was perhaps the most influential business guru of the twentieth century. He died in 2005 at the age of 95. In 1996, as a sprightly 86-year-old, he gave an interview to *Wired* magazine in which he asserted that the computer industry as a whole had never made money: '*Will you people at* Wired *please accept the fact that the computer industry, as an industry, hasn't made a dime?*'[28]

Drucker has often been misquoted as saying the *internet* would never make money, most recently by a former editor of *The Times* newspaper who went on to say, in a graceless and ill-informed piece in *The Guardian* newspaper: '*Most internet-based companies survive on inducing indulgent bankers or governments to spend someone else's money on ventures few of which will make money.*'[29]

It would be interesting to know what Mr Drucker would say about the internet industry had he lived a little longer, accounting, as it now does, for several hugely-profitable major multinational corporations with at least one other waiting in the wings. And that is within 15 years of lift-off. The internet has generated thousands of profitable businesses all over the world and propelled many smaller businesses to profit. We have seen a large number of small businesses launched via eBay and AdWords helping them reach their market in a way that would have been impossible via traditional advertising.

This book has focused mainly on the American and European internet scene. That is because this reflects my own experience of the digital economy, not because what is happening in Asia, Africa or South America is any less interesting. User numbers for the end of 2009 show the BRIC countries (Brazil, Russia, India and China) all appear in the top 10, accounting for about a third of internet users globally.

Country	No. of users	% of world users	Rank
China	360,000,000	20.8	1
USA	227,719,000	13.1	2
Japan	95,979,000	5.5	3
India	81,000,000	4.7	4
Brazil	67,510,000	3.9	5

Country	No. of users	% of world users	Rank
Germany	54,229,325	3.1	6
UK	46,683,900	2.7	7
Russia	45,250,000	2.6	8
France	43,100,134	2.5	9
South Korea	37,475,800	2.2	10

Internet World Stats, November 2009.[30]

We have seen some internet giants emerge in China, including Baidu and AliBaba. In Japan, Yahoo Japan continues to power ahead with its net profit in the *quarter* ended September 2009 exceeding $200m on sales of $756m. These companies may, or may not, have global aspirations; but they are certainly a powerful force to be reckoned with for foreign businesses trying to enter their domestic markets.[31]

We have witnessed too how American online travel company Priceline (Chapter Seven) identified Europe as a major source of growth with its acquisitions of Active Hotels and Bookings.com. In 2007, Priceline made a third online hotel booking acquisition. This time, it was to buy Agoda, based in Singapore, and with operations in Thailand and the Philippines.[32]

Two years after the purchase, Priceline said Agoda was continuing to grow at very significant double-digit rates and that they were very happy with how it was doing so far.[33]

In Latin America there is a social networking war as Google-owned Orkut strives to maintain its dominance over Facebook. Orkut still dominates the Brazilian market: it attracted 22.7 million unique visitors in August 2009, according to Comscore, while Facebook could only manage 1.3 million. But the pressure is on Orkut as, according to Comscore, Facebook overtook Orkut as the market leader in Latin America as a whole in February 2009.[34]

India too has become a battlefield for social networks. Here also Orkut has long been the most popular social network. But apparently Facebook is now closing the gap. By August 2009, Orkut had 15.2 million users versus Facebook's 8.2 million. The important point here is the sheer number of users only in these countries just for two websites: Orkut and Facebook together have over 47 million users – more than the entire population of Spain or Poland![35]

In Africa, which has most of the world's poorest countries, the internet too is enjoying phenomenal growth. By 2009 it had 67 million users, nearly 7% of the population. Compared to the rest of the world, where nearly one third of the population has internet access, Africa still lags, but this will change as costs reduce.[36]

Ethiopia, Ghana, Rwanda and Sierra Leone are participating in the '*One Laptop Per Child Programme*' led by Nicolas Negroponte.[37] Cynics have asked why, in countries where food is scarce, providing cheap laptops should be a priority? The answer to that is that the digital divide is very dangerous and if we do not overcome it, the poor will get poorer and the rich richer.

For those who imagine that the internet is just a fad and that access is just a luxury, like a subscription to a premium cable channel, you have only to look at the research of the World Bank's Aparajita Goyal in India. According to an article in *The Economist* (9 January 2010) this research shows how the internet has helped bring transparency to an agricultural market, making it more efficient, and helping poor farmers to get better prices for their produce.

In the Indian state of Madhya Pradesh farmers had sold their soya beans in auctions to intermediaries, who then sold them on to end-buyers. The problem was that some of these intermediaries allegedly colluded amongst each other to pay less than the market price. So ITC, one of the largest end-buyers of the soya beans, had a brilliant and innovative idea: namely, to set up internet kiosks in villages throughout the region. By the end of 2004 nearly 20,000 such kiosks had been installed.

The kiosks revealed full pricing data and the prices that ITC was prepared to pay. The farmers were now able to check that the prices being offered at the auctions were in line with prices elsewhere. They also had the option to sell their soya beans directly to the end-buyer, cutting out the intermediaries altogether.

Ms Goyal's findings showed just what effect the internet kiosks had had for the farmers: their profits were up 33%, and cultivation of soya beans was up 19%. As for ITC, it covered the cost of the kiosks out of the savings resulting from buying some of the beans directly from the farmers.

This is not the well-publicized internet of Facebook or Twitter or YouTube. It is the internet which, if adopted universally, can quietly make a huge contribution to economic progress and human happiness.

The advertising dollars will continue to pour in

In 2009 the internet was the only advertising medium to grow. Overall global advertising dropped by an astonishing 10% in 2009. The recession has accelerated this trend. As Zenith Optimedia has pointed out, '*in a time when marketing departments have to justify every dollar they spend, the rapid and clear returns offered by internet advertising are more attractive than the longer-term brand-building benefits offered by other media*'.

For anyone working in the digital economy the most recent Zenith Optimedia forecasts give cause for further optimism, pointing to double-digit growth for the next few years. Zenith expects the internet to attract 16.2% of all advertising expenditure in 2012. The gap between internet and newspaper advertising spend has narrowed rapidly. The Zenith Optimedia conclusion is a stark one:

> *We expect the internet to overtake newspapers to become the world's second-largest advertising medium by the time we are half way through the next decade.*[38]

Exceeding the advertising income of the world's newspapers: that would be a nice 20th birthday present for the digital economy.

Afterword

It has never been easier to start a digital business. As Cheapflights' founder Hatt discovered back in 1996, the internet allows you to run a fully-fledged business from your house. The widespread availability of broadband in so many countries means that the audience is there. The cost of building websites has dropped dramatically just as the availability of talent has expanded.

Many of the harsh lessons of the early years have been learned. Digital business is, in many ways, no different from any other business. As Meg Whitman, eBay's former CEO, has observed:

People ask me, how is managing in the New Economy different from managing in the Old Economy? Actually, it's a lot the same. It's about the financial discipline of the bottom line, understanding your customers, segmenting your customers by their needs, and building a world-class management team.[39]

All this is true. As Whitman says, a lot is indeed the same. But it is equally true that a lot is very different. Digital business moves at warp speed. Because there are no bricks and mortar, the barriers to entry are limited. The technology can change with alarming rapidity and digital businesses need to be acutely aware of their ever-changing operating environment.

I have quoted Cheapflights' founder as saying there are only two sorts of internet company: the quick and the dead. Stars that once shone brightly, like AOL, Alta Vista and MySpace and, in the UK,

Friends Reunited, have found this out to their cost. The rapid take-up of the internet outside the USA will mean that the hegemony which it has enjoyed for the first 15 years of the commercial web will be challenged, perhaps in Europe, more likely in Asia. In 1950, the USA had three quarters of the world's car production. Today, it produces fewer cars than China or Japan or the European Union.[40]

For those entering the job market, the digital economy is one of the few bright spots, one of the few sectors which have witnessed growth throughout the global recession. As the change gathers pace, so, increasingly, the best and the brightest will be drawn into the digital revolution. What is feasible today will be trivial tomorrow. I recall my own first sight of a computer. It was in the late 1960s in Strasbourg: an IBM mainframe in a huge air-conditioned room full of men in white coats, like a scene from an early Bond film. Technology was then the preserve of specialists, not the activity of Everyman.

Today, the nerds have indeed had their revenge, surviving the cantankerous criticism of the 'dot.com' collapse to become the rock stars of business. In a sign of our times, the best-selling novels of Patricia Cornwell and Stieg Larsson both have lead characters who are none other than (female) computer whizzes.

This book has shown the lessons that can be learned from the early years of the internet, successes as well as failures. Those early years cannot be written off, as so many have done, as a fiasco. In reality, they were a time when many of today's most successful internet companies were starting out and when users were finding out for the first time – for instance, by searching or by buying – just what the internet could do.

I have shown too that more and more business models are now available to entrepreneurs as users get more sophisticated and the technology advances in line with the take-up of fast broadband. Where once most internet companies based their income on selling advertising banners or things, now the revenue opportunities have multiplied: payment for leads, subscriptions and micropayments, 'freemium' and selling data. But again customers are customers whether they are old economy or new. Customer loyalty and retention in the new economy is just as important as in the old.

I have emphasized the need both to create websites that delight users and to innovate constantly. Coming up with a radically different idea enables you to become a 'market-driving company' which creates a buzz effect that can be very beneficial if well handled. But do be sure to protect your intellectual property with the same energy with which you created it.

Even if the digital economy is moving at a rapid pace and proving itself disruptive to so many traditional business models, that is not a reason for entrepreneurs to ignore the basic commonsense of business over the ages, most importantly the people and the money. Great businesses need great leadership. Simply having a good idea is not enough. Recruiting requires time and dedication. Motivation is much more complex than a simple question of paying people more money. Consider where you locate your office and what your office environment is like, and whether to hire or to outsource. Make sure you get the right advisers, legal, accounting and financial: they can make a big difference. And think carefully about the composition of your board. These business basics will be critical in helping you turn a great idea into a great business.

The money (or rather the lack of it) got so many early dot.coms into trouble. Learn from their failures. Do not raise money unless it is really essential and choose your investors with caution. No business can run properly without effective planning and controls so make sure that you have proper planning processes with sensible budgets. Understand the importance of cash. Especially in harsh economic times cash can be difficult and requires effort. Be very cautious about how you spend your cash. Most entrepreneurs when starting a business will be thinking even then about the exit but be aware: exits are time-consuming and complicated so require a lot of advance planning.

Be careful with your equity. It is a precious resource. But do not forget to allocate options to your team both to motivate them and to make them think as owners rather than merely employees.

Digital media has precipitated a marketing revolution. Exploit word of mouth to the full as well as making careful use of advertising, both online and offline. Public relations can also help accelerate the traffic coming to your website. Be sure that you analyse the effectiveness of your spend.

Ensure too that you maximize the potential of both free (natural) and paid-for (pay-per-click) search. Understand that the rapid expansion of the social networks, especially Facebook, has brought new platforms to gain traffic.

Do not ignore more traditional sources of web traffic such as email and the affiliate model.

I have shown how, despite the global opportunities now available, moving your business across borders presents a minefield and that it is not something that should be tackled in haste.

In sum, while digital businesses have unleashed the need for a whole new series of skills, do not forget the basic business ones which remain essential.

Finally, everyone needs luck. But courage, perseverance and energy too are all vital for success.

NOTES

1 The Digital Revolution – A Short History

1. National Science Foundation, 'Internet/From Modest Beginnings', nsf.gov, 8 January 2009
2. High Beam Research, 'Dot.com Celebrates Its 21st Birthday', highbeam.com, 21 June 2004
3. National Science Foundation, 'Internet/The Launch of NSFNET', nsf.gov, 8 January 2009
4. Berners-Lee, Tim, 'Frequently asked questions', w3.org
5. 'Bad Week For', *The Week*, 17 October 2009, p. 6
6. Sachs, Jonathan, *The Home We Build Together*, Continuum, 2007, p. 67
7. Internet World Stats, internetworldstats.com
8. Nolan, Professor Richard L, Harvard Business School, Cambridge, MA, lecture, 4 June 1999
9. O'Reilly, Tim, Global Network Navigator (GNN), oreilly.com/gnn, August 1993
10. Glasner, Joanna, 'Why Webvan Drove off a Cliff', wired.com, 10 July 2001
11. Virginia Business, virginiabusiness.com, January 2000
12. *Ibid.*
13. Glasner, Joanna, 'Why Webvan Drove off a Cliff', wired.com, 10 July 2001
14. Smith, Chloe, 'ASDA Online Sales up 60% as Web Delivers 35% Growth to £3bn', *The Grocer*, 18 April 2009

15. Goldfarb, Brent, Kirsch, David, Miller, David, 'Was There Too Little Entry During the Dotcom Era?' *Social Science Research Network*, 24 April 2006
16. 'Yahoo! Search Marketing', wikipedia.org
17. Yoffie, Professor David, Harvard Business School, London, lecture, 14 October 2009
18. Tryhorn, Chris, 'The Thoughts of Chairman Mike', guardian.co.uk, 7 March 2007
19. 'Facebook "Cashflow Positive" Signs 300m Users', cbc.ca, 16 September 2009
20. 'The Top 500 Websites on the Web', Alexa.com

2 The Customers – Business Models

1. Sullivan, Patricia, 'Management Visionary Peter Drucker Dies', washingtonpost.com, 12 November 2005
2. Hitwise UK, hitwise.co.uk
3. 'Memorable Quotes for Glengarry Glen Ross', imdb.com, 1992
4. 'Our Journey', EasyJet.com
5. Smith, Oliver, 'Ryanair's Online Check-In Policy: Q&A', telegraph.co.uk, 11 March 2009
6. Lacy, Sarah, 'Your Father's Day Gift Idea: ShirtsMyWay.com', techcrunch.com, 1 June 2009
7. Charlton, Graham, 'Q&A: Peter Crawfurd and Michael Yang of ShirtsMyWay', econsultancy.com, 25 September 2009
8. marketresearch.com
9. Clarke, Jody, 'How I Rode Celebrity Coat Tails to Riches', moneyweek.com, 31 October 2008
10. 2009 Financial Results, asosplc.com
11. 'Asos Dismisses Tesco Fashion Competition', internationalsupermarketnews.com, 17 November 2009
12. Saner, Emine, 'There was a Time When Paying Salaries was Hard ...', guardian.co.uk, 7 May 2009

13. Oldfield, Claire, 'How Asos Defies the Downturn', blogs.bnet.co.uk, 27 April 2009

14. Interview with James Murray Wells, smallbusiness.co.uk, 3 August 2009

15. 'Glasses Direct Backed for £2.9m', growingbusiness.co.uk, 23 July 2007

16. 'Glasses Direct Raises £10 Million', actoncapital.de, 21 April 2009

17. Richardmoross.com

18. Waller, Martin, 'Moonpig has the Rhyme and Reason with Greetings via the Internet', timesonline.co.uk, 7 September 2009

19. Doctorow, Cory, 'Rupert Murdoch Vows to Take all of Newscorp's Websites out of Google ...', boingboing.net, 8 November 2009

20. Hundal, Sunny, 'Exclusive: Guardian Considering Charging for "Members Club"', liberalconspiracy.org, 11 August 2009

21. 'Apple Launches Online Music Shop Offering 99 Cent Songs', brandrepublic.com, 29 April 2003

22. Hargrave, Sean, 'Every Penny Counts', *New Media Age*, 6 August 2009

23. 'About eHarmony Dating', eharmony.co.uk

24. 'match.com', iacadvertising.com

25. PRNewswire, 'IACReports Q2 Results', iac.mediaroom.com, 29 July 2009

26. Dodson, Sean, 'Rune to Move', guardian.co.uk, 11 December 2003

27. 'Jagex's Finances, Ownership, Operation and Trends', runescoop. com, 25 December 2008

28. 'therunescapegroup: Interview with Constant Tedder on BBC Radio 4', youtube.com, 3 June 2009

29. Kincaid, Jason, 'Live Blog: Spotify CEO Daniel Ek Says Music Service Now has 320,000 Paid Subscribers', techcrunch.com, 16 March 2010

30. Andrews, Robert, 'Spotify's Daniel Ek: Why I Believe in a Freemium Model', guardian.co.uk, 21 September 2009

31. Heires, Katherine, 'Why It Pays to Give Away the Store', money.cnn. com, 15 March 2007

32. Lex Column, 'TV Ratings', *Financial Times*, 14 September 2009

33. Internet Advertising Bureau, 'UK Internet Ad Spend Grew 4.6 Percent to £1.75 Billion in H1 2009', iabuk.net, 30 September 2009

34. 'US Online Ad Spend Turns the Corner', emarketer.com, 11 December 2009

35. Schonfeld, Erick, 'JP Morgan Forecasts a 10.5 Percent Rebound in US Display Advertising in 2010', techcrunch.com, 4 January 2010

36. ComScore Press Release, 'Yahoo! Site Ranks as Top Display Ad Publisher in March with 43 Billion U.S. Ad Views ...', comscore.com, 12 May 2009

37. Zuckerberg, Mark, '300 Million and on', blog.facebook.com, 15 September 2009

38. Cain Miller, Claire, 'A Web Start-up Counting on Ad Sales? Good Luck', bits.blogs.nytimes.com, 8 December 2008

39. 'Does Loyalty Pay?', *The Economist*, 23 August 2001

40. Reichheld, Fred, *The Loyalty Effect*, Harvard Business School Press, 2nd ed., 2001

41. Andrews, Fred, 'A Man of Words is Still Partial to One: Loyalty', nytimes.com, 29 December 1999

42. *Ibid.*

43. Hunter, Richard, 'Interview with Fred Reichheld', gartner.com, 24 July 2003

44. Bicknell, David, 'Ten Years of Technology – From Revolution to Evolution', travolution.co.uk, 22 September 2006

3 The Product

1. Kumar, Nirmalya, Scheer, Lisa, Kotler, Philip, 'From Market Driven to Market Driving', *European Management Journal*, Vol. 18, No. 2, 2000

2. Hatt, John, 'A Walking Safari in the Selous', travelintelligence.com

3. Hitwise UK, hitwise.co.uk

4. O'Reilly, Tim, 'What is Web 2.0: Design Patterns and Business Models for the Next Generation of Software', oreilly.com, 30 September 2005

5. Nielsenwire, 'Time Spent on Facebook up 700%, but MySpace Still Tops for Video', blog.nielsen.com, 2 June 2009

6. Simple Thoughts, 'Facebook Tops 10 Most Popular Brands Poll in the UK', blog.taragana.com, 13 May 2009

7. Malmsten, Ernst, *Boo Hoo*, Random House Business Books, 2002, p. 211

8. Nielsen, Jakob, 'Boo's Demise', useit.com, May 2000

9. Malmsten, Ernst, *Boo Hoo*, Random House Business Books, 2002, p. 231

10. *Ibid.* p. 258

11. Burrows, Peter, 'Bezos on Innovation', businessweek.com, 17 April 2008

12. Sviokla, John, 'Innovation Lessons from Amazon', *Harvard Business Review*, blogs.hbr.org, 12 May 2008

13. Pew Internet, 'The Number of Online Adults to use Classified Ads Websites, Such as Craigslist, Has More Than Doubled Since 2005', pewinternet.org, April 2009

14. Kelly, Spencer, 'Craigslist's "Modest Success Story"', bbc.co.uk, 9 March 2007

15. Kumar, Nirmalya, Scheer, Lisa, Kotler, Philip, 'From Market Driven to Market Driving', *European Management Journal*, Vol. 18, No. 2, 2000

16. Berniker, Mark, 'Amazon Sued for Patent Infringement over Personalisation', clickz.com, 18 July 2003

17. Stone, Brad, 'Judge Ends Facebook's Feud with Connectu', *The New York Times*, bits.blogs.nytimes.com, 26 June 2008

18. Arthur, Charles, 'Facebook Paid up to $65 Million to Founder Mark Zuckerberg's Ex-Classmates', guardian.co.uk, 12 February 2009

19. Bricklin, Dan, *Bricklin on Technology*, Wiley Publishing, Inc., 2009

20. *Ibid.* p. 432

4 The Skills

1. Berner, Robert, 'Why P&G's Smile is so Bright', *Business Week*, 1 August 2002

2. Cohen, Adam, *The Perfect Store*, Little, Brown and Company, 2002, p. 111

3. WorkLife Management, 'What is the "Dark Side" of Management?' worklifemanagement.com
4. Moules, Jonathan, 'Finding Funds Need not be Frightening', *Financial Times*, 11 December 2009
5. French-Property.com, 'The French also Live Abroad', french-property.com, 18 August 2009. Paris Talk, 'London, the Seventh Largest French City', paris-talk.blogspot.com, 8 May 2007
6. Guthrie, Jonathan, 'In search of the Next Big Noise amid the buzz', *Financial Times*, 7 June 2007
7. PRNewswire, 'Benchmark Capital Creates Balderton Capital', prnewswire.co.uk, 7 June 2007
8. Soskin, David. 'How to Hire Non-executive Directors', *Growing Business Magazine*, September 2009

5 The Cash

1. Walsh, John, 'Martin Lewis: Money Man', *The Independent*, 28 November 2009
2. Felsted, Andrea, 'Ocado Gets Backing from Al Gore', *Financial Times*, 9 September 2009
3. CrunchBase, 'Facebook', crunchbase.com
4. Cohen, Adam, *The Perfect Store*, Little, Brown and Company, 2002, p. 74
5. Ruddock, Alan, *Michael O'Leary*, Penguin, 2007, pp. 227–230
6. BBC News, 'Ryanair Bans Work Phone Charging', news.bbc.co.uk, 21 April 2005
7. Burrows, Peter, 'Bezos on Innovation', businessweek.com, 17 April 2008
8. Lanxon, Nate, 'The Greatest Defunct Web Sites and Dotcom Disasters', crave.cnet.co.uk, 5 June 2008
9. Garrahan, Matthew, 'News Corp Hit by Office Blow', *Financial Times*, 9 November 2009
10. Ohayon, Ouriel, 'Breaking: Yahoo Finally Sells off Kelkoo', techcrunch.com, 21 November 2008

11. Foxwell, Mark, 'uSwitch's £210m Website "Now Worth Less than £50m"', dailymail.co.uk, 1 August 2009

12. Farrell, Mike, 'Scripps Completes uSwitch Sale', multichannel.com, 23 December 2009

13. Smith, Chloe, 'The Online Crusader: Ocado Finance Chief Jason Gissing', thegrocer.co.uk, 26 July 2008

14. Prosser, David, 'Simon Nixon: Checkout Tills Ringing for Internet Guru', *The Independent*, 9 June 2007. McSmith, Andy, 'The £1 Billion Falling-Out: A Tale of Two Dotcom Millionaires', *The Independent*, 12 July 2007

6 Marketing and Promotion

1. Judge, Elizabeth, 'Nothing Compares to Television's Favourite Meerkat', *The Times*, 4 September 2009

2. Torode, Amelia, 'How a Meerkat Became a Social Media Hero, Creating a Cult Brand', *Admap Magazine*, Issue 508, September 2009

3. quotationspage.com

4. Batelle, John, *The Search*, Nicholas Brealey, 2005, p. 127

5. Cohen, Adam, *The Perfect Store*, Little, Brown and Company, 2002, p. 83

6. Rowan, David, 'eBay's Creation Myth Exposed', *The Times*, 19 July 2002

7. Harding, Matt, 'Where the Hell is Matt?' youtube.com, 20 June 2006
BigglesTheBear, 'Where the Hell is Biggles?', youtube.com, 13 July 2006

8. Hitwise UK: Travel Agency Category, four weeks ending 5 December 2009

9. Google Operating System, 'Google's Market Share in your Country', googlesystem.blogspot.com, 13 March 2009
Marshall, Jack, 'Yahoo Continues to Lose Search Market Share in UK', clickz.com, 29 January 2009

10. Hughes, Tim, 'Expedia "Strikes a Deal with Tripadvisor"', tims-boot. blogspot.com, 22 January 2007

11. PRNewswire, 'Cheapflights.co.uk Tops Natural Search Results in Greenlight Search Study', prnewswire.co.uk, 26 October 2009

12. Batelle, John, *The Search*, Nicholas Brealey, 2005, p. 153

13. Google Press Centre, 'Google Launches Cost-Per-Click Advertising Programme in the UK', google.co.uk, 30 September 2002

14. adwords.google.co.uk

15. Gelles, David, 'Companies Chatter on Twitter to Pack Public Relations Punch', *Financial Times*, 31 December 2008

16. Special Report on Social Networking, *The Economist*, 30 January 2010

17. MediaWeek, 'UK E-mail Marketing Predicted to Rise 15%', mediaweek.co.uk, 13 October 2009

18. Templeton, Brad, 'Origin of the Term "Spam" to Mean Net Abuse', templetons.com

19. Swindonweb, 'Alex Tew: The Kid Done Good', swindonweb.com, 11 May 2009

7 The Rest of the World

1. Hitwise USA

2. NewMedia TrendWatch, 'Over Half of the European Population is Online', newmediatrendwatch.com

3. Google Operating System, 'Google's Market Share in Your Country', googlesystem.blogspot.com, 13 March 2009

4. Speech by Rupert Murdoch, chairman and chief executive of News Corporation, to the American Society of Newspaper Editors on Wednesday, 13 April 2005 quoted in 'Rupert Murdoch: Newspapers in the Digital Age', timesonline.co.uk, 14 April 2005

5. Klein, Saul, 'Why Europe Needs to Seed the Growth of its New Stars?', The Next Web Conference, video.google.com, 2007

6. Cohen, Adam, *The Perfect Store*, Little, Brown and Company, 2002, pp. 188–189

7. Goebel, Markus, 'While other German VC's Wilt, the Samwer Brothers Invest and Clone Like Mad', eu.techcrunch.com, 7 October 2009

8. Butcher, Mike, 'Amazon and Vente-Privee in Talks Over 2 Billion Euro Acquisition, Say Sources', eu.techcrunch.com, 4 December 2009

9. Wauters, Robin, 'Dailymotion Bags another 15 Million Euros', eu.techcrunch.com, 8 October 2009

10. Sjoden, Kerstin, 'Stardoll Takes over Teen Site Piczo', wired.com, 9 March 2009

11. 'Expedia Acquires Europe's venere.com', thedeal.com, 15 July 2008

12. White, Dominic, 'Lastminute Loss Soars to £77m as Costs Spiral', telegraph.co.uk, 26 November 2004

13. Expedia, Inc., Form 10Q, October 2009

14. Priceline, Form 10K, February 2009

15. 'Jeffery H Boyd named President and CEO of Priceline.com', *Business Wire*, 25 November 2002

16. Schaal, Dennis, 'Priceline Overtakes Expedia in Market Capitalisation', tnooz.com, 17 November 2009

17. NewMedia TrendWatch, 'Top 10 Countries Worldwide in Internet Users in September 2009', newmediatrendwatch.com

18. Cohen, Adam. *The Perfect Store*, Little, Brown and Company, 2002, p. 199

19. Toto, Serkan, 'Why Yahoo Japan is Worth Nearly as Much as Yahoo', techcrunch.com, 23 August 2008
Schroeder, Stan, 'When it Comes to Search, Yahoo is Big in Japan', mashable.com, 10 March 2009

20. Amazon Inc., Form 10Q, October 2009

21. JCAST Business News, 'Giant Retailer Amazon.co.jp Shows Continued Sales Growth. Wonder under Business Downturn', en.j-cast.com, 6 October 2009

22. NewMedia TrendWatch, 'Top 10 Countries Worldwide in Internet Users in September 2009', newmediatrendwatch.com

23. Chao, Loretta, 'Yahoo China Dealt Blow', *Wall Street Journal*, 24 August 2009

24. Hong, Iris, 'Google Gains Ground in China's Search Market', businessweek.com, 8 June 2009

25. Barboza, David, 'Google Offers Links to Free Music Downloads in China', nytimes.com, 30 March 2009

26. 'eBay Completes EachNet Investment', investor.ebay.com, 16 July 2003
Barboza, David, Stone, Brad, 'China, Where US Internet Companies Often Fail', nytimes.com, 15 January 2010

27. Blincoe, Robert, 'QXL Shares Going Going Gone', theregister.co.uk, 21 December 2000
Arthur, Charles, 'So Farewell then QXL: It's Been 11 Years, but Someone Bought You', guardian.co.uk, 7 May 2008

8 The Future

1. 'Simon Cowell offers Rage Campaigners Jobs ...', dailymail.co.uk, 21 December 2009

2. Van Grove, Jennifer, 'How Social Media is Changing the Super Bowl', mashable.com, 4 February 2010

3. 'Microsoft Bing Gains on Google, Yahoo in Market Share', chinapost. com, 11 February 2010

4. '36% of Online American Adults Consult Wikipedia ...', pewinter-net.org, March 2007

5. 'Could the Internet Make You Rich?', itv.com, 2010

6. 'The Book of Jobs', *The Economist*, 30 January 2010

7. *USA Today*, 31 December 2009, p. 4B

8. Cane, Alan, 'Leaders Look to Future in Broadband Race', *Financial Times*, 14 October 2009

9. Schroeder, Stan, 'Broadband Internet is Now a Legal Right in Finland', mashable.com, 15 October 2009

10. Metz, Cade, 'Google Chief: Only Miscreants Worry about Net Privacy', theregister.co.uk, 7 December 2009

11. 'Residents Block Google Car', news.bbc.co.uk, 3 April 2009

12. 'Germany's Merkel gives Blessing to Google Street View', dw-world. de, 28 February 2010

13. Harvey, Mike, 'Users Force Facebook to Withdraw Controversial "Copyright" Plan', technology.timesonline.co.uk, 18 February 2009

14. Palmer, Maija, Bradshaw, Tim, Gelles, David, 'Facebook Backtracks on Privacy', *Financial Times*, 12 December 2009

15. Bloxham, Andy, 'Facebook Profile "Could Damage Job Prospects"', telegraph.co.uk, 29 January 2010

16. Coleridge, Nicholas, *Paper Tigers: Latest Greatest Newspaper Tycoons and How They Won the World*, Mandarin, 1994

17. 'Consultation on Legislation to Address Illicit Peer-to-Peer (P2P) File-sharing', berr.gov.uk, 16 June 2009

18. 'Pirate Boss to Make the Web Pay', news.bbc.co.uk, 12 February 2010

19. Donadio, Rachel, 'Larger Threat is Seen in Google Case', nytimes. com, 24 February 2010

20. Watts, Robert, 'Google Pays no Tax on £1.6bn in Britain', technology. timesonline.co.uk, 20 December 2009

21. Parker, Andrew, Taylor, Paul, 'Google Ascendancy Vexes Vodaphone', ft.com, 17 February 2010

22. '2008 Drunk Driving Statistics', alcoholalert.com, 2009

23. Simon, Stephanie, 'When Even Your Phone Tells You You're Drunk, It's Time to Call a Taxi', *Wall Street Journal*, 31 December 2009

24. US Census Bureau, 'State & County Quickfacts', quickfacts.census. gov

25. Office for National Statistics (ONS), 'Population Estimates', statistics. gov.uk, 27 August 2009

26. Lia, Sindre, 'No Less than 54.5 Million Smartphones were Shipped in the Fourth Quarter of 2009, up 39% Year-over-Year', infosyncworld.com, 5 February 2010

27. Ray, Bill, 'Google Navigates Android to Turn-by-Turn Directions', theregister.co.uk, 28 October 2009

28. Schwartz, Peter, Kelly, Kevin, 'The Relentless Contrarian', wired. com, August 1996

29. Jenkins, Simon, 'Palms, Kindles, Nooks, iPads – None are as Cool as Gutenberg's Gadget', guardian.co.uk, 29 January 2010

30. NewMedia TrendWatch, 'Top 10 Countries Worldwide in Internet Users in September 2009', newmediatrendwatch.com

31. Shimamura, Kazuhiro, 'Yahoo Japan Posts 13% Net Profit Gain', online.wsj.com, 27 October 2009

32. PRWeb, 'Priceline.com Acquires Asian Online Hotel Reservations Service Agoda Company', prweb.com, 10 November 2007

33. Hughes, Tim, 'Priceline on Agoda "Agoda had a Very Good Quarter Despite the Fact that They've been Running into Several Headwinds"', tims-boot.blogspot.com, 12 August 2009

34. Cutler, Kim-Mai, 'Battle of Social Networks: How Long can Orkut keep Facebook at Bay in Brazil?', venturebeat.com, 14 September 2009

35. Rao, Leena, 'Facebook's Plan to Trounce Orkut in India may be Working', techcrunch.com, 30 September 2009

36. 'Internet Usage Statistics for Africa', internetworldstats.com

37. 'One Laptop per Child (OLPC)', laptop.org

38. ZenithOptimedia, 'Global Admarket has Stabilised; Prospects for 2010 and Beyond Improving', zenithoptimedia.com, 8 December 2009

39. 'Woopidoo! Quotations', woopidoo.com

40. International Organisation of Motor Vehicle Manufacturers/ Organisation Internationale des Constructeurs d'Automobiles (OICA), oica.net

SELECTED BIBLIOGRAPHY

Anderson, Chris (2006) *The Long Tail: Why the Future of Business is Selling Less of More*, New York: Hyperion.

Battelle, John (2005) *The Search: How Google and its Rivals Rewrote the Rules of Business and Transformed our Culture*, London: Nicholas Brealey.

Bricklin, Dan (2009) *Bricklin on Technology*, Indianapolis: Wiley.

Cellan-Jones, Rory (2001) *Dot.Bomb: The Rise and Fall of Dot.com Britain*, London: Aurum.

Cohen, Adam (2002) *The Perfect Store: Inside eBay*, New York: Little, Brown.

Cringely, Robert (1996) *Accidental Empires: How the Boys of Silicon Valley Make their Millions, Battle Foreign Competitions and Still Can't Get a Date*, New York: Penguin.

Gates, Bill (1995) *The Road Ahead*, New York: Viking.

Kirkpatrick, David (2010) *The Facebook Effect: The Inside Story of the Company that is Connecting the World*, New York: Simon & Schuster.

Kuo, David (2002) *Dot.Bomb: My Days and Nights at an Internet Goliath*, New York: Time Warner.

Loughnane, E (2005) *Net Success Interviews*, Lulu.com.

Malmsten, Ernst (2001) *Boo Hoo: A Dot Com Story*, London: Random House.

Marcus, James (2004) *Amazonia: Five Years at the Epicenter of the Dot.com Juggernaut*, The New Press.

Negroponte, Nicholas (1995) *Being Digital*, New York: Knopf.

Swisher, Kara (1998) *aol.com*, London: Times Books.

Tancer, Bill (2008) *Click: What Millions of People are doing Online and Why it Matters*, New York: Hyperion.

Vise, David and Malseed, Mark (2005) *The Google Story*, New York: Random House.

INDEX